Liberation!

Follow the Book of Hebrews Into a Life of Radical Grace

Dennis McCallum

Copyright 2015 by Dennis McCallum

Visit http://membersofoneanother.com/ for bulk orders and author access

International Standard Book Number 978-0-9836681-9-0

New Paradigm Publishing

Contents

Introduction

Why Hebrews?

In the New Testament, the book of Hebrews stands in the very first rank of importance. With some New Testament books, most of what they teach can be found in other books. Not so with Hebrews. While Hebrews shares some content with other books, large sections are unique and crucial to our understanding of *both* the Old and New Testaments.

Hebrews is also one of the most life-changing books in scripture. No other book more directly challenges conventional religious thinking with such revolutionary, raw grace. Understanding Hebrews is not as easy as understanding most New Testament books, but the effort will be well worth every minute you spend on it, as your eyes are opened in a new way to see the heart of God.

Who wrote it?

Like some other New Testament books, the author of Hebrews never gives his (or her?[1]) name. So, we don't know who wrote it, but we do know a number of things:

- It is a first century book, quoted extensively in the earliest writing by any church father, Clement of Rome. Without debate, Clement wrote around 95 A.D., so Hebrews was written before that.

---

[1] Adolf Harnack thought the author was Priscilla. Adolph von Harnack, "Probabilia uber die Addresse und den Verfasser des Habraerbriefes," (Berlin: Forschungen und Fortschritte, 1900), 1:16–41. That's an intriguing possibility, considering that she was one of the most powerful workers in the New Testament church, was close to Paul, and worked (at last mention) in Rome. If the letter was penned by a woman, it would fully explain why she wouldn't name herself as the author. However, the author uses a masculine self-reference (11:32), which strongly suggests he was a man.

Clement also clearly views Hebrews as scripture, which suggests he thought it was written by an apostle some time earlier.[2]

- The author knew his readers' group. He mentions details about their earlier suffering under persecution (10:32-34). He also reproves them for being too immature to teach (5:11-14), so it was not a new group.

- The author of Hebrews was in the apostle Paul's immediate circle. The author says in Hebrews 13:23, "Take notice that our brother Timothy has been released, with whom, if he comes soon, I will see you."

- The earliest church leaders believed the book was written by Paul. According to Clement of Alexandria (no relation to Clement of Rome) Paul wrote the book "in the language of the Jews" and Luke translated it into Greek.[3] That could explain the similarity some scholars have seen between the Greek style in Hebrews and that in Luke-Acts.

- Although the content and style of the book are unlike much of Paul's other writing, the audience and situation addressed are also different. Greek was a second language for Paul, but to fellow

---

[2] I find very unconvincing the argument (from silence) that because the temple isn't specifically mentioned in Hebrews, the book must have been written after the destruction of the temple in 70 A.D. This argument is invalid, not only because it includes no positive evidence, but because Old Testament passages on the tabernacle provided the entire biblical instruction for ritual in the temple. Therefore, the extensive concern about how the tabernacle works really points to a date when the temple was still in use. Otherwise, why take so much interest in temple rituals that no longer exist? Also, on what else would the author ground an argument about the theology of ritual and covenant? We have no Old Testament teaching on temple ritual that applies only to the temple but not the tabernacle. References in Hebrews to people who "crucify to themselves again the son of God" (6:6; also 10:26) probably mean that some of the readers are performing ongoing ritual sacrifice in the temple. This would place the book earlier than 70 A.D., when the temple was destroyed.

[3] We don't have Clement's own text (*Hypotyposes*) on this, but Eusebius' quotation of him in Eusebius, *History of the Church* 6.14.2–3. Historians believe this is an accurate quotation of Clement's work, which was still in existence up until the ninth century, according to other readers. Eusebius also claimed that Origin accepted Clement's view. Also, the very important late second-century papyri, P[46], a volume of Paul's epistles, includes Hebrews right after Romans.

Aramaic-speaking Jews he would be in position to strongly unload his vast understanding of the Old Testament scriptures with a new level of eloquence.

- Paul had a bad reputation with many Christian Jews, according to James (Jesus' half brother). In Acts 21:20-21 they told him, "You see, brother, how many thousands there are among the Jews of those who have believed, and they are all zealous for the Law; and they have been told about you, that you are teaching all the Jews who are among the Gentiles to forsake Moses, telling them not to circumcise their children nor to walk according to the customs."

They proceeded to arrange for Paul to engage in some vow-keeping ritual at the temple in order so that "all will know that there is nothing to the things which they have been told about you, but that you yourself also walk orderly, keeping the Law" (v. 24).

These doubts about Paul's view on Old Testament law raise important questions answered finally and clearly in the book of Hebrews. This book calls on Jews and all Christians to forget about following the Mosaic covenant and accept that the new covenant under Jesus renders the former rituals obsolete.

Interestingly, Paul never completed the offering James had arranged, because the crowd identified and attacked him before he could do so. Some interpreters wonder whether Paul's move to engage in temple ritual would have been a mistake on his part, and therefore God kept him from completing it. If so, Paul may have had a shift in thinking himself, and the letter to the Hebrews could be the result. That might also explain why Paul would not name himself as the author as he does in his other books. He may have felt the book would have a better chance of acceptance if he left himself out of it and just cited scripture.

- Arguments that Barnabas or Apollos may have written the book carry some plausibility, but the fact remains that the early church accepted the book as scripture because they believed Paul wrote it. Whoever actually wrote it, Paul is the apostolic authority behind the book. He may have had one of his co-workers write it with him (notice the "us" and "we" in 13:18), or it could have been translated from an Aramaic original as Clement claimed (which would help explain the more fluid and eloquent style).[4]

So, we conclude that the book was probably from Paul or one of his close colleagues. Also, Paul is the apostolic authority behind the book.

Audience and destination

The book had a title, "To the Hebrews," from the earliest times. The oldest manuscripts we have all include that title, and we have no good reason to strike it down. Most commentators agree that the book is obviously written to a community of Jewish Christians. The content of the book makes perfect sense if written to such a group in which people still looked to the old covenant. On the other hand, much of the content would seem out of place if addressed to a Gentile group.

Most commentators think the destination was Rome, but lack convincing reasons for that conclusion. The only real argument for this destination is that Clement of Rome knew the book and quoted it extensively. But is this really proof that the destination was Rome? I don't think so.

First, if the letter was written *from* Rome, that would explain why the church in Rome had it at an early date. We know early churches made copies of each other's apostolic letters, and they may have done so with this one. Clement of Alexandria's suggestion that Hebrews was translated into Greek would make sense here: they would have sent the Aramaic original east and kept their Greek translation in Rome.

---

[4] Guthrie covers the various arguments well, but like most commentators, he concludes that Paul is not the author, had nothing to do with writing the book, and that the destination for the book was Rome. Donald Guthrie, *Hebrews: An Introduction and Commentary* (Grand Rapids: Wm. B. Eerdmans Publishing, 1983) 27ff.

If the letter was written *to* Rome, why would the author say to believers in Rome, "Those from Italy greet you" (13:24)? It's more natural to think the author is writing *from* Italy, unless we accept the suggestion that a group of Italian Christians had moved somewhere else.[5] Why would a group of Christians from Italy move somewhere else? Where did they move? Why would the author call them "those from Italy" if they now lived elsewhere? This proposal seems forced, and the only rationale seems to be a desire to hang on to the Rome hypothesis.

The idea that we can identify the destination of a book by who quotes it in the first century is flawed because we have almost nothing from that period. In fact, Clement of Rome is the only extra-biblical Christian author we have who is definitely from the first century, so our earliest extra-biblical material is extremely fragmentary. If we don't have a single letter from anyone in any other church in the first century, why think that others didn't know the book as well? We simply cannot determine a book's destination this way.

We know that later in the second century, Hebrews was well-known in the eastern empire, but less so in the west. Christians in Rome continued to view Hebrews as an important canonical book, but others in the west began to question it, mainly because the author is not named. This again suggests that Hebrews was sent to the eastern empire and copies of it spread from there.[6]

I agree with earlier commentators that this book is written to Jewish Christians in Judea; probably in Jerusalem. This is the same group we read of in Acts—a group that had exhibited amazing spiritual vitality during the early years, but began to lose their way as decades passed. In fact, more than thirty years after Jesus' ascension, most members in the group were probably second-generation. They were withering under persecution and drifting back toward the full practice of ritual Judaism. In the midst of this

---

[5] This is argued by many commentators, including Leon Morris, Donald Guthrie, D.A. Carson and others. But I think entirely too much weight is being put on his use of *apo* (from) instead of *eis* (in). Either word would be a natural way to describe people currently living in Italy.

[6] R. Laird Harris, *The Inspiration and Canonicity of the Bible,*(Grand Rapids: Zondervan, June 1971) 276.

crisis, Paul (or one of his helpers) took pen in hand and wrote this amazingly deep and powerful call to radical grace.

The battle in Hebrews

At the heart of Hebrews is a thesis set against an antithesis. The author is battling a particular concept: that following Jesus can be domesticated under formalism and legalism. The particular form of legalistic teaching current in this ancient group involved a blend of rabbinic ritual Judaism and a weakened form of following Jesus.

This could take other forms today, but the message remains as relevant as it ever was. The compromise evident in these readers was so serious it could imply complete apostasy—a falling away from the gospel—leading to spiritual death. Whenever such legalism rears its head, we must wonder whether its followers ever truly grasped the nature of God's grace in Jesus.

The battle between legalism and radical grace has raged since ancient times. During most of those centuries, and in most places, legalism has gained the ascendency. Self-righteous, controlling, and dangerous, legalists haven't hesitated to attack. They persecuted Jesus and his followers from the earliest days, including the readers of Hebrews. The book is a plea to understand what's at stake, to persevere under persecution, and to stay faithful to the one message that causes more trouble than any other—radical grace.

The proud natural human hates radical grace. Legalistic thinkers simply cannot stand hearing grace's repudiation of human pride and plain declaration of human helplessness. Like the people who covered their ears and ran screaming at Stephen (an early champion of grace) with murderous fury (Acts 7:57), people today still hurl themselves at those who dare to take God at his word.

Some readers today completely miss the point of Hebrews. We see a terrible irony when the book of Hebrews, instead of breathing liberating grace, becomes a storehouse of legalistic threats. Shockingly, some interpreters mistakenly conclude that the very perspective Hebrews warns against is the one we should adopt!

As a faithful reader, you need to examine the train of thought in this book and draw the conclusions intended, not those that accord with your tradition.

Jews and Christianity

The argument in Hebrews is not between Judaism and Christianity. Properly understood, Christianity *is* Judaism. Or we could say that Judaism, properly understood, *is* Christianity. True Judaism is of God and from God, so Christians should never speak against it. The problem addressed in Hebrews is a faulty understanding of what true, biblical Judaism teaches.

True Judaism under the covenant of Moses was an important stage in God's plan for humanity—a plan that culminates in Jesus. As we will see, both Old and New Testaments agree on that fact. Some Jews don't want to hear that today, just as some didn't want to hear it back then, but "the stone the builders rejected became the chief cornerstone" (1 Peter 2:7). A key message in Hebrews is that following Jesus is not compatible with holding on to one's popularity with the neighbors, especially the legalistic ones.

At the time Hebrews was written, thousands of Jews had seen the truth of Jesus, just as hundreds of thousands see that today. Hebrews has in fact been an invaluable guide helping many Jews see how their background from Moses leads naturally and almost inescapably to the gospel of Jesus.

Early Christian Jews faced serious difficulties. Imagine yourself having been raised under a strict rabbinic understanding of the scriptures. Your whole life you've observed kosher laws, kept the festival calendar, offered sacrifice at the temple, and avoided assorted forms of evil.

Then Jesus came. You probably never sat directly under his teaching, of if you did, it was probably only very little. You might have seen him perform a miracle or know somebody who did. You didn't see him after his resurrection, but again, you have heard from others who did. You realize he is the Messiah and place your faith in him.

As a Jewish Christian, the question of the relationship between Jesus' revelation and Moses' revelation is paramount. Over a period of years, you've arrived at a synthesis that honors both.

But now comes the even more difficult part. It's one thing to trust that Jesus is the Messiah, but this Hebrews author is suggesting that the synthesis you and your friends worked out isn't good enough. Instead of a compromise, he thinks virtually everything you've ever learned as an observant Jew is now obsolete.

According to Hebrews, none of the rabbinic teachings you have trusted since your youth are right, and now must be rejected. Instead of going to temple as you've done since childhood, this writer thinks you should never go there again. He thinks you should break with everything your neighbors think is appropriate in a way that is very likely to incite hostility, just as you saw in earlier years.

What will it take for the author of Hebrews to make this case? Clearly, it won't be easy.

For one thing, you're not going to accept anything based on some person's opinion. You know the books of Moses, the prophets, and the Psalms are inspired of God. If you're going to listen to any new theology, it will have to be proven based on the one authority you accept: scripture. Yes, you respect Jesus, but you see no reason to think that anything he taught is contradictory to the scriptures you've been nurtured on all your life.

And that's exactly how our author plays it. From first to last, Hebrews breathes the Old Testament scriptures. This book delves into the heart the old covenant like no other book. Without Hebrews, we would be guessing in one area after another how Old and New Testament revelation relate to one another. But Hebrews removes all ambiguity, in fact showing that anyone who respects the Old Testament scriptures must accept the view Hebrews advances.

Chapter 1: The question of authority

Who says?

Before you can lead people to a conclusion—especially one they might not want to hear—you have to establish what is authoritative. You need to recognize any common ground, and make clear the basis for accepting any new material.

That's where Hebrews begins. The author's first proposition is, "God has spoken!" This is common ground between the readers and the author, but an important point to restate at the beginning. Who is our authority when it comes to spiritual matters?

In our world today, people feel they have the right to make up their own religion based on what feels right to them. Back then, tradition held a comparable place. People might not be able to detail all their beliefs from scripture itself, but they knew what their rabbis had taught them, and they knew what their families had always done for worship. Thus they, like many Christians today, didn't base all their views on scripture. Instead, they had a mixture of tradition and scripture.

But Jesus rejected the old wineskins of rabbinic tradition because he knew they would never hold his new wine (Luke 5:37-38). Similarly, our author isn't going to base his argument on tradition at all. Rather, he points out that God "spoke long ago to the fathers in the prophets in many portions and in many ways" (1:1). The Old Testament scriptures are from God according to this, and therefore they are authoritative. Scripture, not tradition, must call the tune in our thinking.

But then comes the punch line: "In these last days [he] has spoken to us in His Son" (1:2). If prophetic visions and dreams were authoritative, how much more is revelation that comes from God's own son? This is an *a fortiori* argument that follows the form, "If this, how much more that?"

Indeed. How much more? Much more! Jesus was nothing less than a personal visit from God. To appreciate the new level to which God raised revelation, these readers need to remember who the son is.

Who is Jesus?

Our author declares:

> ...His Son, whom He appointed heir of all things, through whom also He made the world. And He is the radiance of His glory and the exact representation of His nature, and upholds all things by the word of His power. When He had made purification of sins, He sat down at the right hand of the Majesty on high. (Hebrews 1:2-3)

The readers of Hebrews may have already accepted these things about Jesus, because the author doesn't defend them. As King Messiah, he would be the heir of all things. Consistently throughout Hebrews, the author takes for granted that his readers believe Jesus is the Messiah. But have they connected the dots fully when it comes to the incarnation? Did they realize that Jesus was the agency of all creation? Did they fully realize he was the exact representation of God's nature and the radiance of his glory? Judging from the argument in chapters 1 and 2 there's room for doubt. At least, they seem to have let slip from their thinking the full implications of these things.

They do seem to believe in Jesus' atoning death. At several places in the book, the argument assumes they already believe it, but again, they may not have completely connected the dots. One implication is clear: Since he is seated at God's right hand, whatever Jesus says must have supreme authority.

Angels?

Then, abruptly, we read, "having become as much better than the angels, as He has inherited a more excellent name than they…" (1:4). Nine verses follow comparing and contrasting Jesus with angels. Why are we reading about this? What's the point?

The point is that, according to rabbinic teaching, the entire Old Testament was transmitted by angels. The Jews revered the books of the Old Testament in part because God cared enough to send angels with the message. Our author doesn't deny the logic of that view; he simply points out that if angels deserve respect, how much more does God's son?

Again, he is not questioning the authority of the Old Testament books—far from it; his argument comes from the Old Testament itself. A crucial part of the argument in Hebrews is that the Old Testament prophets always saw the Sinai covenant as temporary and would be superseded by a new order brought in by the promised one.

The prophecies of the Old Testament themselves declare the absolute superiority of God's son over the angels. To demonstrate this, our author sets forth six examples:

1. In Psalms 2:7 God says, "You are my son, today have I begotten you." God never said such a thing about any angel.[7]

2. In 2 Samuel 7:14 God announces the so-called Davidic Covenant, including a reference the rabbis always understood to refer, not only to Solomon, but ultimately to the Messiah: "I will be a father to him and he will be a son to me."

3. In Psalms 97:7 God says through the Psalmist, "Let all God's angels worship him." Angels are never to be worshipped, and they never worship anyone but God.

4. In Psalms 45:6-7 as our author correctly sees, when the Psalmist says, "God, your God has anointed you," he is referring to the Messiah.

---

[7] An exception here is "the angel of the Lord." When given with the definite article like this, the expression refers to Jesus before his incarnation. This is not an angel in the usual sense, but a usage of the word angel in the more general sense as a messenger. See examples where "the angel of the Lord" is clearly God in Genesis 16:7, 9–11; 48:15–16; Exodus 3:2–6; 23:20–23; Judges 6.

5.   In Psalms 102:25-27 the one laying the foundation of the
     earth must refer to the Messiah because of the context of the
     messianic age in verses 21-22.

6.   Finally, when David refers in Psalms 110:1 to both God and a
     coming one—whom he addresses as "my Lord" (Adonai)who
     will sit at God's right hand until his enemies are like a
     footstool for his feet—this must refer to the Messiah who is
     here addressed using one of the common Old Testament
     words for God.

Since his readers already accepted that Jesus was the Messiah, these
passages (some of which were also considered messianic in rabbinic
teaching) require that they also view Jesus as creator, ruler, and indeed as
God. So, respecting angels is no reason to miss the more important point:
The son deserves even more respect.

The big picture

In Chapter 1 of Hebrews, our author has already painted his readers into a
corner. Yes, they respect the Old Testament books as inspired by God. But
have they noticed that those very books predict a Messiah who is none other
than God in human form? They cannot honestly look at messianic passages
in their own Bible without accepting that once God's son came, every
previous revelation was superseded.

Thus, the authority question is answered: the new authority in revelation is
Jesus—not that he opposes or negates the old authority, but that he was
always anticipated and pre-authenticated by the very scriptures he
supersedes.

Notice that this view is no oddball claim found only in Hebrews, but the
consistent testimony of the whole Old and New Testaments. When Jesus
was here he plainly stated that he had authority from the Father to change
everything (John 5:26-27). When the Pharisees charged his disciples with
breaking Sabbath law, Jesus deconstructed their charge, but in the end gave
the more salient point: "The Son of Man is Lord of the Sabbath" (Luke 6:5).
With a few comments, he overthrew scores of Old Testament verses and

"declared all foods clean to eat" (Mark 7:19). He said he was greater than the prophets (Matthew 12:41-42). He argued that a proper understanding of Moses and the prophets shows they were writing about him the whole time (John 5:46).

How much of this had the readers of Hebrews already realized? Was it that they didn't comprehend the obvious truth about Jesus? Or was it that they didn't want to look at these truths because they had become inconvenient?

We can't be sure because, as we will see, when someone hardens his heart against God, it powerfully affects his ability to comprehend spiritual truth. Anyone who sets out on a path of sin could quickly be blinded even to truth he earlier understood. As Jesus warned, "For whoever has, to him more shall be given, and he will have an abundance; but whoever does not have, even what he has shall be taken away from him" (Matthew 13:12).

The question of Jesus' authority is just as pressing in our day as it was for the ancient Hebrews. Professed Christians all over the western world today have relegated Jesus to a position of even less authority than had the readers of Hebrews. First comes what we "have to do" (i.e. the things of the world), then some "me time," and whatever is left over is for Jesus—unless something comes up.

Only a clear view of Jesus in his transcendent sovereignty will arrest our hearts and result in a correct view of God's revelation. And unless we grasp that lofty revelation, we will constantly tend to bring Jesus' call down to a level that fits with our cultural assumptions, just like the readers of Hebrews were doing.

Chapter 2: Jesus, our leader in submission

Knowing the truth and following it are not necessarily the same thing. Our author goes directly to the point in Chapter 2:

> For this reason we must pay much closer attention to what we have heard, so that we do not drift away from it. For if the word spoken through angels proved unalterable, and every transgression and disobedience received a just penalty, how will we escape if we neglect so great a salvation? (vs. 1-3)

This section implies that the readers were "drift[ing] away" from what they had heard, and "neglect[ing]" the gospel. It's clear they had been taught the truth at one time. They must have rationalized their new position, either not realizing how far they had drifted, or refusing to think about it. Humans have a remarkable ability to do what we want even if what we want contradicts everything we believe.

He reminds them of another confirmation of the message:

> After it was at the first spoken through the Lord, it was confirmed to us by those who heard, God also testifying with them, both by signs and wonders and by various miracles and by gifts of the Holy Spirit according to His own will. (vs. 3-4)

Jesus also stressed that his miracle working verified his authenticity when he said, "The works which the Father has given Me to accomplish—the very works that I do—testify about Me, that the Father has sent Me" (John 5:36).

This passage clearly shows that the readers of Hebrews had witnessed miracles at the hands of apostles, which in turn argues that this is the Jerusalem group that grew out of Pentecost. What better description could you imagine for that group who saw the miracles described in the early chapters of Acts? And how many groups in other cities could be described as seeing miracles from multiple apostles?

But many commentators think the opposite. They think this verse shows that the readers are second generation Christians who came to faith decades after Jesus' life, because he doesn't refer to them receiving the message from Jesus himself. Many of them probably were second generation—more than thirty years had passed since Jesus' resurrection.

But even people living in Jerusalem during Jesus' ministry needed the apostles to explain what had happened. When we see Peter telling the crowd about the resurrection on Pentecost, we also see the crowd was comprehending it for the first time as the message "was confirmed to [them] by those who heard." But the author even implies some of them had heard the message from Jesus himself when he says "it was at the first spoken through the Lord."

Secondly, some argue that this passage speaks of the apostles as a distant memory. That's not necessarily true—only that they preceded the author (because he lumps himself in with the "us" instead of "them"). If we think about Paul's biography, this fits well. Unlike other cities where Paul could argue that he was their first source for hearing the gospel, Jerusalem heard it from other apostles before Paul was a believer, and he heard it from those same apostles when he came to Jerusalem after his conversion.

Some interpreters also think this passage proves the author of the book is not Paul, because he says "it was confirmed to *us*." Paul, they argue, makes it clear that he got his gospel directly from Jesus (Galatians 1:12). But in that same passage, Paul said he did compare his gospel with the gospel Peter and the other apostles taught:

> I submitted to them the gospel which I preach among the Gentiles, but I did so in private to those who were of reputation, for fear that I might be running, or had run, in vain. (Galatians 2:2)

But he had not run in vain. His message was the same as theirs.

> And recognizing the grace that had been given to me, James and Cephas and John, who were reputed to be pillars, gave to me and

> Barnabas the right hand of fellowship, so that we might go to the
> Gentiles and they to the circumcised. (Galatians 2:9)

In other words, James, Cephas, and James "confirmed" what he already had
heard, just as Hebrews 2:3 says. Paul could easily have made this statement.

So, Jesus had been confirmed to the readers through his own miracles and
other miracles they saw performed through the apostles. By now, it was
clear that Jesus' authority was established through Old Testament prophecy
and through his miraculous works. This is where the division between our
modern chapter one and two should be (after 2:5) instead of where it
currently is. From here, our author leaves the topic of why Jesus is our final
authority and moves on to discuss his work.

Priesthood

In contemplating his audience, our author must have realized that they
didn't fully understand who Jesus is, or what he did. For instance, abundant
evidence in Hebrews shows that they did not understand that Jesus
completely fulfills the Old Testament role of priest. This was evident from
the fact that they were continuing to accept the legitimacy of Levitical
priests. Our author knew that if he could make the case that Jesus is the only
valid high priest today, his readers' legalism (associated with their trust in
traditional priests) would become untenable.

This argument is so important that it runs for several chapters. Once we
admit that all high priestly functions now exclusively belong to Jesus, other
conclusions must follow like a line of dominos falling, where the first is the
priesthood of Jesus.

Sovereign humility

To make his readers understand the full impact of what Jesus did, our
author now goes into so-called reversal theology. Jesus introduced this
when he taught that whoever is great in the world will be least in the
kingdom but whoever humbles himself like a child will be great (Matthew
18:1–4). He said that which is highly valued among men is despicable to
God (Luke 16:15). In a word, God's values overturn all the wisdom that
fallen humans hold to.

Jesus truly showed God's reversed values by living them. Paul stresses of Jesus that, "though He was rich, yet for your sake He became poor, so that you through His poverty might become rich" (2 Corinthians 8:9). He was the one who "did not regard equality with God a thing to be grasped, but emptied Himself, taking the form of a bond-servant, and being made in the likeness of men. Being found in appearance as a man, He humbled Himself by becoming obedient to the point of death, even death on a cross" (Philippians 2:6-8). Jesus reversed his right to be worshipped and glorified so that our fair condemnation to the sentence of hell would also be reversed in our acceptance by God.

Here in Hebrews, our author stresses the same point. The irony of love is that God would even care about humans, let alone abandon his position in heaven to become one. This again, is all foretold in the Old Testament:

> What is man that you remember him? Or the son of man that you are concerned with him? You have made him for a little while lower than the angels; you have crowned him with glory and honor, and have appointed him over the works of your hands; you have put all things in subjection under his feet. (Hebrews 2:6-8, quoting Psalm 8:4-6)

This is a complicated passage, both here in Hebrews and in its original context in Psalms. Commentators' opinions abound. One of the main problems is the possibly vague referents of the pronouns "he" and "him". Our author's follow up observations narrow the meaning: "For in subjecting all things to him, He left nothing that is not subject to him" (v. 8b). Here, he seems to be stressing the meaning of "all things."

Then he says, "But now we do not yet see all things subjected to him" (v. 8). By observing that humans do not now have all things in subjection, he points out an added dimension in this Psalm.

> But we do see Him who was made for a little while lower than the angels, namely, Jesus, because of the suffering of death crowned with glory and honor, so that by the grace of God He might taste death for everyone. (v. 9)

How does Jesus get into this passage? Is it the reference to "the son of man" in verse 4 (so there is "man" and "the son of man")? This is tempting, but doesn't seem to match the meaning in Psalm 8, where both man and the son of man refer to humans. Could it be that before humanity can achieve God's plan for it, there must be redemption? That Jesus must lead the way in bringing humanity to a place of final victory? Yes! But reversal theology teaches that, for God, the way up is down. Before Jesus was crowned with glory and honor, he volunteered to descend into humanness and suffering.

The incarnation

In the incarnation we have the most extreme and hard to believe claim in the Bible. Parting the Red Sea or walking on water look like nothing compared to this astonishing claim: the almighty creator God put himself into a human body and lived as a man! As John puts it, "The Word became flesh, and dwelt among us" (John 1:14).

> For it was fitting for him, for whom are all things, and through whom are all things, in bringing many sons to glory, to perfect the author of their salvation through sufferings. (Hebrews 2:10)

Here our author puts God's glorious nature next to Jesus' humiliation and suffering. His humiliation was not the self-immolation that comes out of ascetic thinking. Jesus emptied himself and became human for a purpose— to rescue people. It also made intimacy possible between a holy God and sinful people.

In the next three verses, the author cites Old Testament passages that refer to brotherhood, saying that Jesus was "not ashamed to call them brethren; I will proclaim your name to my brethren, in the midst of the congregation I will sing your praise" (vs. 11-12). These verses come from Psalm 22, which *is* a messianic psalm. Before the Lord could refer to people as his brethren, incarnation was necessary—an act that brought the son into the midst of the people he would rescue.

The incarnation made adoption possible. According to the New Testament, we are the adopted brothers and sisters of Jesus. This is a teaching not found in the Old Testament. Although God said he was like a father to the nation of Israel a couple of times, the teaching that believers are adopted children of God (let alone brothers with Jesus) awaited the coming of Christ. He taught us to pray "our father," a way of addressing God found nowhere in the Old Testament scriptures.

The reference to Isaiah 8:13—"I will put my trust in him... and the children whom God has given me"—seems not to be a fulfillment of any messianic passage, but more like an allusion to a perspective that Jesus had in common with Isaiah. But whereas Isaiah had his children via procreation, Jesus acquired his through incarnation and adoption.

This leads to one of the most important passages in the New Testament on the incarnation:

> Therefore, since the children share in flesh and blood, He Himself likewise also partook of the same, that through death He might render powerless him who had the power of death, that is, the devil, and might free those who through fear of death were subject to slavery all their lives. (vs. 13-14)

Here is a key reason why incarnation was necessary. Jesus' work couldn't be done from heaven. In fact, it could only be done by a human. Jesus occupied multiple, complex roles when he came. One of the most important was that of priest. But here, the focus is more on his role as sacrifice—as the one who out-died all deaths. The dark background of spiritual war, evident in many New Testament passages, rears its head here.

Why did Jesus have to overcome Satan's power of death by dying? This is a complex question, and we don't know the full answer. Clearly, there are rules at work—judicial principles based on God's character. These are constraints on what God can do because of his own self-consistency. God can't simply decide to look the other way regarding human evil and pretend it didn't happen. His just character requires that a punishment be paid, and from day one, he announced to Adam that death would be the sentence for sin (Genesis 2:17).

Another rule appears to be that a representative for humans must be human—and not just superficially human. Jesus had to be human all the way down.

> Therefore, He had to be made like His brethren in all things, so that He might become a merciful and faithful high priest in things pertaining to God, to make propitiation for the sins of the people. (v. 17)

How could Jesus be like his brothers "in all things"? Isn't that a bit exaggerated? After all, he was still the son of God.

We can't press the expression "all things" too far. Jesus was not like other humans in every single way. For instance, we have no evidence that he had a sin nature like we do, and Romans 8:3 implies he did not (because he was "in the likeness of sinful flesh" rather than "in sinful flesh"). He also remembered his preexistent life with the father (John 17:5), which is different than us. This verse means he was fully, not partially, human.

Yet Jesus did demonstrate surprising limitations:

- He said he didn't know when he would return (Matthew 24:36), which flatly contradicts the omniscience of God, as does the statement in Luke 2:52 that Jesus "grew in wisdom." God never grows or learns.

- Mark records that "He could do no miracle [in his hometown] except that He laid His hands upon a few sick people and healed them" (Mark 6:5). Such inability contradicts the omnipotence of God.

- Jesus didn't manifest omnipresence. For instance, in John 4:4 we read, "And He had to pass through Samaria."

- Jesus was tempted by Satan, even though James says God can't be tempted (James 1:13).

- We see Jesus growing hungry (Luke 4:2) and tired (John 4:6). This contradicts God's self-existence, whereby he has no needs.

So we see Jesus living out of his humanity, even though he was divine. How much of his life came from his humanity, and how much came from his divinity? Our best evidence is that Jesus limited himself to living *entirely as a man*. He was full of the Holy Spirit, and this enabled him to perform miracles, just like it did for his disciples after him. In fact, everything Jesus did during his life could be explained by the power of the Holy Spirit.

It wasn't that Jesus didn't *have* his divine attributes, but that he apparently didn't *access* or *use* them during his life on earth. Instead of living as God, Jesus lived a life of complete dependence, drawing everything from God. He said, "The Son can do nothing of Himself" (John 5:19).[8]

So we have a paradoxical picture of Jesus. On one hand, Paul can say that "in Him all the fullness of Deity dwells in bodily form" (Colossians 2:9). But at the same time, he lived "like his brothers in all things."

Jesus' emptying of himself and humiliation were extreme. He voluntarily turned away from using his power and limited himself to what any other human could do through the power of the Holy Spirit. We read that "the Lord's healing power was strongly with Jesus" (Luke 5:17), and Peter said, "God publicly endorsed Jesus the Nazarene by doing powerful miracles, wonders, and signs through him" (Acts 2:22). This is why Jesus said, "He who believes in me, the works that I do, he will do also; and greater works than these he will do" (John 14:12).

Why would Jesus live exclusively out of his humanity? The answer has to do (at least in part) with the rules governing priests and sacrifices, as we just read: "He had to be made like His brethren in all things, so that He might become a merciful and faithful high priest in things pertaining to God, to make propitiation [i.e. satisfaction] for the sins of the people." As both human and divine, Jesus is the perfect mediator between us and God. But if Jesus had gone beyond his human nature while living his life, he

---

[8] Opinion is divided over the exact extent of Jesus emptying himself. Wayne Grudema, for example, thinks Jesus had two "centers of consciousness," one of which had limited knowledge, while the other "clearly knew all things." This takes us into areas of mystery that have not been revealed. The passages he uses to back up this claim are questionable. For instance John 2:25 "He did not need anyone to testify concerning man, for He Himself knew what was in man," doesn't teach omniscience. It teaches that Jesus had an accurate view of human nature. John 16:30 and 21:17 don't really say Jesus was omniscient either; both are spoken by followers and are general statements about his insight. The language we use for Jesus' two natures could easily lead to error. Grudem might be right, but all we can say for sure is that Jesus never spoke of these two centers of consciousness. I think it's best to stick with what scripture reveals and avoid rationalistic extrapolations. There is clearly much we don't know about how Jesus' two natures worked, but the Bible says he lived as a man.

probably would not have been suitable as our substitutionary sacrifice, or as our high priest.

Sympathy

Our author shares one last comforting thought in verse 18: "For since He Himself was tempted in that which He has suffered, He is able to come to the aid of those who are tempted."

Jesus suffered. He felt the agony of temptation. He was sickened by the presence of sin, rejected by friends and family, and in every way experienced the difficulty of living in a fallen world, just like we do, but worse. This is an important point and one of the key themes in the book of Hebrews. People under legalism conceive of God wrongly. They often see him as sullen, disgusted, and angry. Some end up with a view of God little different than a brain in a jar—emotionally detached from us. Naturally, you don't feel too safe getting close to this kind of God. The lack of confidence one feels in approaching such a God is one of the key symptoms of legalism. When believers understand Jesus' love and sympathy, they can approach him with confidence, or boldness.

Chapter 3: From faith to a hardened heart

Jesus and Moses

The early Jewish Christians had a high view of Old Testament revelation because it was transmitted by angels, as we've seen. But they also revered Moses, the human agent of revelation for the Pentateuch. It's hard for modern readers to grasp how much ancient Jews admired Moses. He was their national hero like no other. According to the Jewish Encyclopedia, "He occupies a more important place in popular legend than the Patriarchs and all the other national heroes."[9]

The Pentateuch itself made Moses' teaching the standard for what counts as valid revelation. In Deuteronomy 13:1-5, Moses made it clear that any contradiction to his teaching was clear proof of false prophecy, punishable by death. To the view of ancient Jews, any call to go in a radically different direction from what Moses taught was very difficult to accept. Only powerful proof could convince them God was moving in a new direction. This leads to a comparison and contrast between Jesus and Moses. Our author points out that Jesus "was faithful to him who appointed him, as Moses also was" (3:2), so they were alike in that regard.

But Jesus "has been counted worthy of more glory than Moses by just so much as the builder of the house has more honor than the house. For every house is built by someone, but the builder of all things is God" (3:3-4). When you stop to see an innovative house designed by Frank Lloyd Wright, it's the architect that you admire, and you admire him through his work.

---

[9] Some of the lore developed around Moses is funny, but it gives an idea of the high view accorded him by ancient rabbis: He was born already circumcised He spoke with his father and mother on the day of his birth, and prophesied at the age of three. Pharaoh's daughter had leprosy, but on touching Moses was cured. At 3 years old, he took the crown from Pharaoh's head and placed it on his own. He was proclaimed king by the Ethiopians, and he ruled over Ethiopia for forty years. While in heaven receiving torah… God taught him also everything which every student would discover in the course of time. "Moses" in *The Jewish Encyclopedia* www.jewishencyclopedia.com. Of course, none of these claims are true or based on scripture.

God is the creator, and Jesus was God in human form. This strong passage on the deity of Christ must be a great embarrassment to cult groups who deny his deity, even while claiming they believe the New Testament is inspired.

The point in the argument here in Hebrews is similar to the one in Chapter 1: Moses deserves respect for what he did and who he was. But when the son of God comes into the picture, everything changes. Jesus and Moses are not on the same level. Rather, Jesus is the culmination of everything Moses wrote, as our author is about to demonstrate.

Had the readers already accepted the deity of Christ? There must be doubt. They would have known Jesus had no human father, but the Jewish view of God was so transcendent that to this day devout Jews are scandalized by the Christian claim of the incarnation. Nothing is harder for devout Jews to accept.

The inertia of unbelief

The real problem with the readers was not their theological upbringing. It turns out that their incredulity came from a moral, not an intellectual source. This kind of unbelief results from something called "hardening your heart."

Psalms 95 first alludes to an event where God's people's need for water and thirst was setting in. They began to attack Moses, blaming him for failing to supply water. They put the worst interpretation possible on the crisis—that he had brought them from Egypt only to see them slain in the desert (Exodus 17:3).

In this case, their need was legitimate, and in due course God met it with water from a rock. But the fact that their needs were legitimate didn't excuse their blasphemous charges against God and his delegate, Moses. This was the first of no fewer than *ten* similar revolts, finally culminating in an event that caused God to declare them all over the line.

The author quotes Psalm 95:

> Today, if you hear his voice, do not harden your hearts as in the rebellion, as on the day of testing in the wilderness, where your ancestors put me to the test. (Hebrews 3:7-9)

Here, our author is still quoting Psalm 95, but the psalmist is referring to a different episode described in Numbers 13-14. In this story, Moses had led the people up to the southern boundary of the promised land, to a place called Kadesh Barnea.

Before entering the promised land, Moses sent twelve spies ahead to spy out the land for forty days. They hiked all over Canaan and confirmed that it fully lived up to the billing Moses had given it. They reported to the assembly, "We came to the land to which you sent us; it flows with milk and honey, and this is its fruit" (Numbers 13:27). Then they showed off a grape cluster so large they had to sling it on a pole between two men!

However, they went on, there's a problem:

> The people who live in the land are strong, and the towns are
> fortified and very large; and besides, we saw the descendants of
> Anak there. The Amalekites live in the land of the Negeb; the
> Hittites, the Jebusites, and the Amorites live in the hill country;
> and the Canaanites live by the sea, and along the Jordan.
> (Numbers 13:28-29)

And they added,

> We are not able to go up against this people, for they are stronger
> than we… The land that we have gone through as spies is a land
> that devours its inhabitants; and all the people that we saw in it are
> of great size. There we saw the Nephilim (the Anakites come from
> the Nephilim); and to ourselves we seemed like grasshoppers, and
> so we seemed to them. (Numbers 13:31-33)

Not everyone agreed. Two of the spies, Joshua and Caleb, argued that they could take the land because God had promised it. But the majority sided with the pessimistic spies.

Before jumping to conclusions, we should note that what the ten skeptical spies said was far from nonsense. These nations they named were powerful and numerous. Even God described them as "seven nations larger and stronger than you" (Deuteronomy 7:1). The "Nephilim" they refer to were apparently a very large race of people, who would be highly dangerous in hand-to-hand combat.

The Jews, on the other hand, were an escaped group of slaves. They had never learned to use weapons, and had only fought one battle against some raiders. Unlike the warlike peoples in Canaan, who fought battles every year, they knew they were poorly prepared for armed conflict. They had no base from which to manufacture weapons, or knowledge of how to do so. How to overcome fortified cities must have been a complete mystery to these people. If each of the seven nations in Canaan was larger than all of Israel, as Deuteronomy 7 says, then they were contemplating walking into a situation where they would be outnumbered by perhaps ten to one!

So, from the military and practical point of view, the skeptical spies made sense. Their observations were not insane, but they were missing something: God played no part in their analysis. In their view, on one hand Israel is this size, and on the other hand are the Canaanites at ten times that size. The two are a complete mismatch.

The dynamic nature of unbelief

We now know from Psalms 95 that leaving God out of their calculations was an act of rebellion against God. Joshua and Caleb pointed this out at the time in Numbers 14:9 where they said, "Only do not rebel against the Lord!"

We can virtually guarantee, however, that this was not how the 10 cautious spies viewed their position. To people caught up in sin and unbelief, it never seems like rebellion: "Rebelling against the Lord??!! We're not rebelling against God. We just don't want to be shredded by a bunch of over-sized Nephilim! We don't want our wives and children to become slaves (Numbers 14:3). That's not rebellion; it's just common sense! Haven't you guys noticed how outnumbered we would be? Don't you realize we have nothing for besieging walled cities?"

The faith God expected in this situation was not like New Age mind power. New Agers think they can believe whatever they want and it will happen if they believe hard enough. The Israelites had God's word on this situation. God had spoken through Moses and validated his word with a series of the most extreme miracles. The whole story up to this point was about God calling his people to leave Egypt for a promised land. Joshua and Caleb were exactly right: to leave God out of the calculation like these spies were doing was to ignore a colossal series of divine actions and even the audible voice of God.

But hearing God speak from a mountain and believing he will work in a potentially dangerous military situation are different things, especially when potential suffering is involved. Unbelief is easy to rationalize and hard to recognize in yourself at first. It's not only subtle when it comes; it is also progressively corrosive.

At one moment, they were just trying to assess their chances against superior foes. Soon, they were wailing, arguing that they might as well all be dead, accusing God of wanting them dead, claiming that their families were going to become plunder, and that they should remove Moses from leadership, take over, and head back to Egypt (14:1-4). What began as some seemingly common-sense observations quickly exploded into murderous, blasphemous despair.

Unbelief is a slippery slope. If God isn't going to keep his word in one area, it's hard to see why he would keep it in another area. Unbelief at *any* point really implies the reasonableness of unbelief at *every* point. Satan knows how this train of thought works, because it's a trail he's been down himself. Unfortunately, he's very good at guiding believers down the same path.

The hardened heart

The readers of Hebrews were sliding down this very slope. Surrounded by hostile neighbors and a dangerous government, it was probably easy to begin wondering how far they really needed to go in breaking with ritual Judaism. By all accounts, Jesus hadn't clearly spelled this out in his teaching, and a little bit of accommodation might go a long way in diffusing tensions.

At first, they may have merely gone along with some marginal practices at the temple that didn't involve blood sacrifice. Perhaps they cut down on how many times a week they went to Christian fellowship gatherings. Maybe some of them began discussing how necessary it was to be so "different" as Christians. At some point, their inner eyes went from trusting God to trying to fit in—staying under the radar.

But unbelief comes to unbelief. Soon, a compromise that seemed minor was expanding into other areas. Something began to happen in their hearts that made it harder to see the danger. Their hearts were being hardened. Hardening of the heart is subtle, gradual, and very difficult to detect from inside the heart being hardened. If one compromise makes sense, why not another very similar one? Before long, the compromises were piling up and they found themselves very far from where they began.

At the same time, their hardening heart caused them not to see what was happening; it made them scowl at the idea of being too hard-line or narrow. What was to be gained by taking a line of interpretation that alienates people? Like the people in Numbers, they probably felt anger at those who hadn't joined them in their compromise. When Caleb and Joshua pleaded with them, Numbers 14:10 records that the skeptics actually wanted to stone them to death!

"Today"

Hardening of the heart can sneak up on people, but it's not too late to get back into a right relationship with God. The author of Hebrews calls our attention to the word "today" in Psalms 95:7. The word sounds a note of hope: although things may have disintegrated spiritually, that doesn't mean they were doomed. At any moment they could have their eyes opened and change their hearts.

Referring to the story of Kadesh Barnea, our author says,

> Take care, brethren, that there not be in any one of you an evil, unbelieving heart that falls away from the living God. But encourage one another day after day, as long as it is still called "Today," so that none of you will be hardened by the deceitfulness of sin. (Hebrews 3:12-13)

The "deceitfulness of sin" refers to the way a hardened heart sneaks up on people. With anything this dangerous, they need to "take care." Our author implies that they can help each other to see the way to repentance. When I can't see what's happening in my life, fellow believers in my community might see and have the love—and the guts—to call me back to full trust.

Although these readers stand on a precipice, in clear danger of missing God's rest, this is still "today." Tomorrow might be too late! For the sinful spies and their followers at Kadesh, it was too late. The day they spread their rebellion to the other people, God decreed that all of them must die. It doesn't mean they were condemned to hell, but they could no longer be a part of God's program. They could no longer change their minds about entering the promised land.[10] With unbelief, you never know when you might reach a limit with God.

This could happen to us. We might suddenly and unexpectedly experience physical death—a sure limit that blocks any change of heart. We might do damage to ourselves so severe it can't be repaired. Or, we could reach a level of hardness that becomes final, where nothing can budge our rock-hard hearts. But right now, today, it's not too late.

And so we see the significance of "today." If you find God speaking to you, it means there's at least one more chance. How urgent it becomes to flee the devastation of the wilderness of unbelief: "Today if you hear His voice, Do not harden your hearts."

The penalty of unbelief

What was the penalty for the unbelief at Kadesh? God recalls in Psalms, "I swore in My wrath, 'They shall not enter My rest'" (Hebrews 3:11). In their

---

[10] Hebrews 3:14 warns, "For we have become partakers of Christ, if we hold fast the beginning of our assurance firm until the end." Many take this verse to be a warning that those who turn to unbelief will lose their personal salvation. Yet, as we'll see, the author of Hebrews is adamant that forgiveness isn't doled out day by day as needed. Rather, we are forgiven "once for all." So God doesn't need to wait and see whether we will remain faithful before he knows whether to finally bestow salvation. God knew all about people's unfaithfulness when he bestowed grace in the first place.

At the same time, a careful analysis of the book shows that the author is unsure how many of his readers are authentic believers. Considering the way they were falling away from grace, it seemed possible that some of them never truly came to know the Lord. This doubt about their true spiritual state accounts for the ambivalent language in several passages in Hebrews. He isn't threatening them with losing their salvation; he may be calling into question whether they ever really had it.

Another way to read this passage is that they are in danger of losing their place in God's program of reconciling the world to himself (2 Corinthians 5:18-20). To those who truly know Jesus, not being used by God is a horrifying possibility. Notice that the word here for "partakers" (*metoxoi*), usually carries the meaning partnership, or having something in common. It often describes business partners. As those who have had the word of reconciliation "committed to us," we can never be truly fulfilled unless we are "God's fellow workers" (1 Corinthians 3:9).

case, this meant physical death for the entire generation (except for Joshua
and Caleb). The readers of Hebrews didn't face physical death, but they
might still fail to enter God's rest. Dutch Reformed author Andrew Murray
explains:

> Some think that the rest of Canaan is the type of heaven. This
> cannot be, because the great mark of the Canaan life was that the
> land had to be conquered and that God gave such glorious victory
> over enemies... This is the rest into which [one] enters, not through
> death, but through faith.[11]

When the next generation of Israelites entered Canaan, they had to fight, but
the fighting was supernaturally empowered. The very foes they feared so
much at Kadesh melted away before the power of God, just as he had
promised. Instead of laboring in futile weakness under their own strength,
they now accessed the power of God.

The penalty facing the readers of Hebrews was a future struggling under
legalism and missing the liberating freedom of grace in Jesus.
Compromising with legalism kills spiritual vitality, because the legalist is
no longer living in faith.

No privileged class

It was probably hard for these Hebrew Christians to accept the idea that
they might miss what was theirs in Christ. After all, they came to Jesus first.
Before that, they were the bearers of God's torch through the old covenant.
They had Moses, the ultimate man of God, as their teacher. All other early
Christian groups took their lead from the Jewish church in the early
chapters of Acts. And now they're supposed to accept that they are far off-
base?

Our author reminds them that they wouldn't be the first insiders to lose it:

> Who provoked Him when they had heard? Indeed, did not all
> those who came out of Egypt led by Moses? (Hebrews 3:16)

---

[11] Andrew Murray, *The Holiest of All: Exposition of the Epistle to the Hebrews*, Second Edition, (Ipswich, EN:
James Nisbett & Co. 1885), 144.

That was one of the most privileged generations in history, but what good did it do them? Even after the astonishing parting of the Red Sea, there they were, condemned to wander aimlessly until dead. For the readers of Hebrews, this is an important reminder: The Jews at Kadesh also had Moses as their leader. Just because God worked through a group at one time means little about whether he will continue to do so.

This would be a good point for modern Christians to reflect on. Do we feel that we've arrived? Are we self-satisfied in our worship experiences and our lovely churches? The danger we're reading about in Hebrews 3 is a clear threat to every Christian group, not just the weak ones. As soon as we begin to feel superior, it's usually a sign that legalism is taking hold. When we feel alienated and distant from God, it's usually a sign that we gauge our access to him based on our works. People slipping under law have dark secrets about their sin and are unwilling to confide in anyone.

Maybe the readers of Hebrews were trusting their well-being to accommodation with their Jewish neighbors. We might trust our wellbeing to accommodation with our secular, materialistic neighbors. We may not think of our careerism as a turning away from God, even though we have far less excuse for our defection from God's values than they did.

What's the answer when you feel your spiritual sensitivity and zeal slipping away? You have to understand what entering God's rest means today.

Chapter 4: There remains a rest

Studying Old Testament stories like the failure at Kadesh is interesting, but how do we know they apply today? In Chapter 4, our author shows how entering God's rest is not just for the early Israelites. The principles involved are basic to all true faith.

> So we see that they were not able to enter because of unbelief. Therefore, let us fear if, while a promise remains of entering His rest, any one of you may seem to have come short of it. For indeed we have had good news preached to us, just as they also; but the word they heard did not profit them, because it was not united by faith in those who heard. (Hebrews 3:19-4:2)

Clearly, the author thinks entering the promised land still has application fifteen hundred years later. In the verses to follow, he proves that this is not his invention, but was David's intention in the Old Testament text.

> For we who have believed enter that rest, just as He has said, "As I swore in my wrath, they shall not enter my rest," although His works were finished from the foundation of the world. For He has said somewhere concerning the seventh day: "And God rested on the seventh day from all his works." (Hebrews 4:3-4)

This passage confuses many. Why does he begin talking about God resting on the seventh day of creation in the context of Numbers 14? Simply put, it's a word study. Comparing Numbers' and Psalms' treatment of the same incident, our author sees the term "my rest" coming up. He has gone to the first use of the expression in scripture to learn what the concept of God's rest is supposed to teach. This takes him to Genesis 1 and a very good question: Why would God need to rest after the six days? Surely an omnipotent being doesn't need rest. And here we find the key. God didn't *need* to rest. There was only one reason for his rest: his work was finished. Notice his reference to this in verse 3, where he says that God rested "although His works were finished from the foundation of the world." Here we have the first hint of the subject that will dominate the rest of the book: the finished work of Christ.

This isn't midrashic interpretation (the word-association, hidden meaning approach seen in later ancient rabbinic writing). He is simply arguing that when God speaks of rest, the reason is not weariness. The reason God rests is that work is no longer necessary; everything is done. So the basis for us to enter God's rest is the same: Jesus has finished all the needed work.

In the next verses our author shows that he has not invented this expanded definition of God's rest. It was already expanded in Old Testament scripture that his readers accepted as inspired.

> Therefore, since it remains for some to enter it, and those who formerly had good news preached to them failed to enter because of disobedience, He again fixes a certain day, "Today," saying through David after so long a time just as has been said before, "Today if you hear his voice, do not harden your hearts." For if Joshua had given them rest, He would not have spoken of another day after that. So there remains a Sabbath rest for the people of God. (Hebrews 4:6-9)

He is showing that the notion of entering God's rest must have meaning beyond the original story, because David is still warning people not to miss God's rest hundreds of years after the Kadesh story in Numbers. God "fixes a certain day, 'Today,' saying through David after so long a time...." David is telling his readers that if they adopt the same attitude of unbelief, they will miss the chance to enter God's rest, just like those at the time of Moses.

Our author points out that "if Joshua had given them rest," David wouldn't still be talking about entering God's rest hundreds of years later. He has linked Genesis 1, Numbers 14, and Psalm 95 to show that the idea of entering God's rest is broader than this one incident at Kadesh. His reasonable conclusion follows: "So there remains a Sabbath rest for the people of God" (Hebrews 4:9).[12]

---

[12] It should also be clear that the author is committed to a historical-grammatical reading of the Old Testament. His lesson here comes in large part from the historical sequence and chronology of Moses, Joshua, and David, combined with a word study on the idea of God's rest. Again, this is not midrashic interpretation.

If the idea of entering God's rest was still valid in David's day, then it must be a timeless concept that applies in different forms to every age. And our author explains the heart of the concept in verse 10: "For the one who has entered His rest has himself also rested from his works, as God did from His."

Either one thing or the other

In Hebrews 4:10 we almost have the thesis of the whole book summarized in one sentence. "For the one who has entered His rest has himself also rested from his works, as God did from His."

Good work needs to be done. People are alienated from God and headed for judgment. Sin ravages individuals and whole societies. Who will repair this situation? The biblical answer is clear: Jesus Christ. The important point is that Jesus has already acted and that action is sufficient. What believers need today is not to add to Jesus' work, but to appropriate it by faith.

The readers of Hebrews needed to understand the finished work of Christ. They clearly believed Jesus was important, but also felt that adding human works to Jesus' work was a good thing. They didn't suspect that adding human works really amounted to unbelief, but it does. We can't trust the finished work of Christ, and at the same time feel we need to add our own works. Adding our works clearly suggests that Jesus' work isn't good enough.

Works then and now

Think about the unbelieving spies at Kadesh. They looked at the fearsome enemies in Canaan as something they had to overcome. They didn't view it like Joshua and Caleb, who believed God would handle these enemies if the Israelites just showed up in faith. Interestingly, under both views, they had to show up and draw swords to fight. The difference is really one of motivation and power source. Under a true grace perspective, we act in serving God, but with two crucial caveats: (1) We believe that when we act, God will perform the work. Our power to perform comes directly from God. (2) We don't act in order to be accepted and blessed. Instead, we act *because we are already* accepted and blessed (Ephesians 1:3).

Thus, entering God's rest is an inward matter. The question isn't mainly what we do, but how and why we do it. That's why, in the thought progression of this passage, the author goes on to point out,

> The word of God is living and active and sharper than any two-edged sword, and piercing as far as the division of soul and spirit, of both joints and marrow, and able to judge the thoughts and intentions of the heart. And there is no creature hidden from His sight, but all things are open and laid bare to the eyes of Him with whom we have to do. (Hebrews 4:12-13)

Passages of scripture like these throw back the blanket, revealing the inadequacy of legalistic thinking. They expose the deepest need in the heart of all believers: real trust of God that leads to "bold access." People who seize God's offered rest begin to experience joy and victory in the Holy Spirit. This is the faith/rest walk where Jesus' finished work becomes the all-sufficient basis for everything we need.

That's why the author speaks of revealing "the motives of men's hearts," and of all things being "open and laid bare" before God's eyes. Our author isn't calling on his readers to enter into some new discipline or to try harder. Rather, what they need is faith—faith that Jesus' finished work is adequate, and adequate not only for personal salvation, but for growth, ministry, and everything else. The readers need faith that God will take care of them, and that they don't need to return to a works-based religion in order to get by.

Entering God's rest is when we throw off every hope from self-effort and self-sufficiency and finally and fully begin to trust.

Working to rest?

Verse 11 says, "Therefore let us be diligent to enter that rest, so that no one will fall, through following the same example of disobedience." The Merriam Webster Dictionary defines 'diligent' as "characterized by steady, earnest, and energetic effort." NIV translates, "Let us, therefore, make every effort to enter that rest...." NLT reads, "do our best" to enter. How is this rest?

All these translations are for the Greek word *spoudazo*, a word that should be translated in this context, "zeal." The semantic range of *spoudazo* spans from working to being zealous, so the question is which meaning fits this context best. It's not that we work to enter God's rest, but that we need to be zealous—focused and urgent—to not miss the opportunity. Abundant evidence shows that the trend in this Hebrew church was in the opposite direction.

Chapter 5: Understanding priests

Centuries before Jesus, God handed down a system of ceremonial law to Moses. This collection of rules for festivals, objects, and ceremonies allowed illiterate people to see and learn spiritual principles about God. They illustrated truths about God's relationship with humans, and his plan for the world. Instead of reading texts, they would enact something like spiritual dramas illustrating key themes—especially the future work of Christ. Jesus said, "If you believed Moses, you would believe me, for he wrote about me" (John 5:46). When did Moses write about Jesus? The whole ritual system he taught was foreshadowing Jesus from first to last.

The author of Hebrews now explains how the whole Bible is a carefully crafted explanation and prediction of what Jesus did. First, he focuses on the central role of priests in the worship system in Moses' law.

At the center of the coded message in the tabernacle is the idea of *separation*. Scripture teaches that humans are sinful and God is "holy." The holiness of God means he is different from us. Sinful people are so different from God that we cannot just waltz into his presence as though nothing were amiss. God is morally offended by sin, but at the same time, he loves humans (John 3:16).

To resolve this paradox, God introduced the role of intermediary—priests. Worshippers were not allowed to approach God directly at the tabernacle. They needed to bring their offerings to the priest, who would take it and approach God with it. Unlike church buildings today, the tabernacle was not a place where people gathered for singing and preaching. Only the priests went into the tabernacle itself; the people stayed out in the waiting area in front (which also had no seats).

The tabernacle (and later the temple, which was built on the same design) stood for where God lives—his house and throne room in heaven. It was also designed to picture our problem with God and his solution. The problem is sin. His solution is substitution—instead of the guilty worshipper going under God's judgment, a sacrificial animal dies in his or her place. Then, priests presented the offering to God.

In the law we see two main types of priests: regular priests and high priests. The high priest conducted the offerings on the Day of Atonement described in Leviticus 16 and 17. During this holy day, the high priest took blood from an animal sacrifice signifying all the sins committed by Israel that year. He carried it into the inner sanctum called "the Holy of Holies" and displayed it there. This was the premiere picture of God's people obtaining forgiveness and satisfying God's justice.

Rules

When reading about these rituals, one is struck by the detail and specificity in the instructions. God gave instructions involving hundreds of details covering every aspect of the environment and actions prescribed. Through such detail God was signifying this: God can be approached, but only on his own terms. By specifying how the people and the priests were to conduct themselves when relating to him, God ruled out all innovation or creativity. God is fine with creativity and innovation, but not when approaching God for forgiveness. If the people innovated, it would suggest that they could devise their own ways of approaching God, and that would imply coming to God based on our own works.

Humans prefer to dictate how we come to God, and our ideas nearly always involve us doing something to buy God's favor. But God won't allow that, and in fact, it's an insult. When humans think we can pay God off with some good works, it just shows that we don't understand how bad our sin problem is or how righteous God is. That's why the tabernacle rituals stress that only substitution stipulated by God—where an innocent dies in place of the guilty—can satisfy God's justice. And even that substitution has to be presented indirectly through a priest.

Today no less than then, God stipulates how we may approach him. For the readers of Hebrews to develop their own hybrid way to come to God was completely out of the question.

Jesus' priesthood

In the book of Hebrews, we learn that Jesus has now become the one and only valid high priest. Instead of going to a human priest, we now go to Jesus. Instead of regular offerings, his was once and for all time. As we already saw, Jesus' work is finished. And because of that work, we have access to an amazing closeness to God:

> Therefore, since we have a great high priest who has passed through the heavens, Jesus the Son of God, let us hold fast our confession. For we do not have a high priest who cannot sympathize with our weaknesses, but One who has been tempted in all things as we are, yet without sin. Therefore let us draw near with confidence to the throne of grace, so that we may receive mercy and find grace to help in time of need. (Hebrews 4:14-16)

Here is the burden of Hebrews. If we want to go on to maturity in Jesus, we must develop the ability to approach God "with confidence" or "with boldness" as some versions translate. Under legalism, people cower before God, never completely sure where they stand with him. Only under the absolute security that our new high priest brings can we run to God with the confidence and boldness that a child feels when running to his or her father.

Comparing and contrasting

In the next few verses, our author points to several parallels between Jesus and earlier high priests.

1. A high priest must be a human being. "For every high priest taken from among men..." (5:1). The reasons for this are never explicitly revealed, but apparently the rules governing how intercession works require that humans be represented before God by a human. Therefore, Jesus' incarnation was not optional.

2. High priests are in charge of offering sacrifices to God. "Every high priest is appointed ...in order to offer both gifts and sacrifices for sins" (5:1). So, Jesus had to bring his own sacrifice to God in heaven.

3. "He can deal gently with the ignorant and misguided, since he himself also is beset with weakness" (5:2). Priests share in human nature and are therefore sympathetic with worshippers.

4. "And because of it [his weakness] he is obligated to offer sacrifices for sins, as for the people, so also for himself" (5:3). Human priests had to undergo a cleansing ritual before they could do their work. A so-called laver, or wash basin, was part of the tabernacle for this purpose. Jesus, on the other hand, didn't need this washing, because he was without sin.

5. "And no one takes the honor to himself, but receives it when he is called by God, even as Aaron was" (5:4). Priests aren't like dentists, who decide what they want to do as a profession. God declared who the original high priest would be and whose descendants would carry that work on. Again, this system is not set up with freedom to innovate. God chose Jesus to be the final and permanent high priest.

Why Jesus could not be a priest

The idea that Jesus is our high priest was very hard for the audience of Hebrews to accept. In fact, it flies directly in the face of key biblical teaching in the old covenant.

First, all Jewish priests had to come from the tribe of Levi. That is clearly stated in the law of Moses. Jesus, however was not from that tribe. He came from the tribe of Judah, a tribe appropriate for kings but never for priests. So this is a non-starter for the Jewish readers of Hebrews.

Even if some solution were found to the tribe issue, these readers would have another reason they could not accept the Jesus' chief priesthood. When any chief priest either died or reached the age of sixty, another priest would be chosen to succeed him. These readers would wonder, "How could Jesus be our priest when he isn't here anymore? Who are we supposed to go to at the temple?"

The answer, of course, is that they shouldn't be going to the temple anymore. But imagine how difficult that would be to accept for people who had worshipped this way all their lives. Accepting the proposition that Jesus has now permanently replaced all high priests, and that the temple itself is no longer of use to believers would require ironclad proof from the only source they would respect: holy scripture.

Notice that while Jesus hinted at the changes in view here, he never clearly spelled them out.[13] Instead, we learn about Jesus' priesthood from the book of Hebrews—and the Old Testament.

Why Jesus is a priest

Our author has anticipated these objections and now gives the solution. We already saw that just as the Jews weren't permitted to innovate in the way they worship, neither were they empowered to decide who would be priest. God reserved that decision to himself.

Our author goes on,

> So also Christ did not glorify Himself so as to become a high priest, but He who said to Him, "You are my son, today I have begotten you" just as He says also in another passage, "You are a priest forever according to the order of Melchizedek." (Hebrews 5:5-6)

This notion of a priesthood of "the order of Melchizedek" was unclear to the readers. Although it was right there in Psalms 110, the passage doesn't make that much sense until you connect all the dots and see the subsequent history of Jesus. Let's start at the beginning.

Melchizedek

In very ancient times, around 2000 years before Jesus, we read of a military raid on the city of Sodom, where part of Abraham's family lived. Genesis

---

[13] For instance, when he told the woman at the well that "an hour is coming when neither in this mountain nor in Jerusalem will you worship the Father" (John 4:21), he implied that the whole system of worship from the old covenant was about to be overthrown. But the statement is very general. Again, the challenge, "Destroy this temple, and in three days I will raise it up" (John 2:19), hinted that his body would replace temple worship. But, as John points out, even his followers didn't understand what it meant at the time (v. 22).

14 reports that a king named Chedorlaomer and his allies "took all the goods of Sodom and Gomorrah and all their food supply, and departed. They also took Lot, Abram's nephew, and his possessions and departed, for he was living in Sodom" (vs. 11-12).

When Abraham heard about the raid, he mounted a successful counter attack and was able to free Lot and his family, also recapturing all the booty they had taken. Journeying back through Israel to Sodom, in the south, he and his men met two kings. One was the deposed king of Sodom, who must have escaped during the battle. He was happy to see his citizens and their treasure coming back. The other was our man, Melchizedek: "And Melchizedek king of Salem brought out bread and wine; now he was a priest of God Most High" (Genesis 14:18).

Immediately something should catch our attention. This man is called "a priest of God Most High," but there's a problem: the Old Testament office of priest *didn't even exist at this time*! Moses, through whom God set up the Levitical priesthood, wouldn't appear for another 600 years.

How strange that the biblical text wouldn't say Melchizedek *thought* he was a priest, or that he *claimed* to be a priest. Rather, it is clear he was a priest, and he was also the king of Salem, an earlier name for Jerusalem. So, he was a priest-king. Other oddities appear in the story as well. First, the name Melchizedek means "King of righteousness." Also, his title, king of Salem, means "King of peace." So he is introduced as the king of righteousness and peace.

In the interaction that follows, it becomes clear that Abraham accepts Melchizedek as his priest and spiritual superior. This is clear first because Melchizedek blesses Abraham. "He blessed him and said, 'Blessed be Abram of God Most High, Possessor of heaven and earth; And blessed be God Most High, Who has delivered your enemies into your hand'" (vs. 19-20). In ancient custom, for Abraham to receive this blessing at the hands of Melchizedek means that he recognized Melchizedek as his priest. This recognition is confirmed in the next line when he donates a tenth of the battle spoils, "He [Abraham] gave him [Melchizedek] a tenth of all" (v. 20). For Abraham to tithe to Melchizedek is another indication that Melchizedek is over him as a priest.

And that's the end of the story.

Any careful reader must find this short account very intriguing. First, Abraham was a man very close to God. God had already spoken to Abraham directly more than once. Why would he need to submit himself to the priesthood of this stranger? Shouldn't Melchizedek be the one on his knees receiving a blessing from Abraham?

Also, who is this man? He appears suddenly and without explanation. We see no family history or list of connections that make him great. Usually, people in the Old Testament have some genealogy that explains why they are important. And yet, despite his apparent lack of pedigree, it is clear that Abraham recognizes Melchizedek as his intercessor with God.

What does this have to do with Jesus?

By inference, if Melchizedek out-ranked Abraham spiritually, he also out-ranked Abraham's descendants. In ancient thinking, one must respect his elders, so Abraham, who was an elder to the later priests, like Aaron, is to be respected above them. Yet Melchizedek is above Abraham!

The readers of Hebrews knew Jesus was the Messiah, but how could they know he was a priest? If only there were a way to connect the office of King Messiah to a priesthood similar to Melchizedek, we might have a solution to the quandary mentioned earlier—that Jesus was not from the right tribe to be a priest. But Melchizedek wasn't from the tribe of Levi either. He wasn't even Jewish. Yet, he was a priest, and a very important one. At the very least, this episode opens the possibility that other priests might exist besides the Levitical priests.

David to the rescue

A thousand years after the encounter with Abraham, another biblical author took up his pen and mentions Melchizedek for the only other time in the Old Testament. The text is Psalm 110, and it begins,

> The Lord says to my Lord:
> "Sit at My right hand
> Until I make Your enemies a footstool for Your feet."
> The Lord will stretch forth Your strong scepter from Zion, saying,

> "Rule in the midst of Your enemies."
> Your people will volunteer freely in the day of Your power;
> In holy array, from the womb of the dawn, `
> Your youth are to You as the dew. (vs. 1-3)

Here we see David saying "The Lord (*Yahweh*) says to my Lord (*Adonai*)...." This is a strange statement considering that David was an absolute monarch. *Adonai* is a word that can be used of God or of human overlords. But who would David call his *Adonai*?

As the context develops, the answer is clear. This is a future king (notice the reference to his royal scepter in verse 2), and it's king Messiah. From the earliest times the rabbis considered this a messianic psalm.[14]

But the punch line comes next:

> The Lord has sworn and will not change His mind,
> "You are a priest forever
> According to the order of Melchizedek." (v. 4)

Well, well, well! Isn't this amazing? Here, with one verse of scripture (and an earlier three-verse story), we have an open and shut case for the priesthood of Messiah.

Notice also the term of office: "Forever." So the other problem (that Jesus is no longer on earth) is also solved. This kind of priest doesn't get replaced, he is an eternal priest-king. And according to the readers of Hebrews' own beliefs, Jesus is Messiah.

Because of the superiority of Melchizedek, any Levitical priest would have to step aside in deference to this loftier order of priest.

---

[14] Notice Jesus calling attention to the same point in Mark 12:35-37: "As Jesus was teaching the people in the Temple, he asked, 'Why do the teachers of religious law claim that the Messiah is the son of David? For David himself, speaking under the inspiration of the Holy Spirit, said, "The Lord said to my Lord, Sit in the place of honor at my right hand until I humble your enemies beneath your feet." Since David himself called the Messiah "my Lord," how can the Messiah be his son?'" Interestingly, the rabbis had no answer to his query, because they did not have clear understand of this Psalm.

The big picture

We pointed out earlier that only irrefutable biblical proof would move the readers of Hebrews to abandon the temple system on which they had been raised. Here is that very proof! By causing an event in 2000 BC and inspiring a psalmist in 1000 BC, God had anticipated the problem and solved it in advance.

Bible skeptics should ask themselves how they think a string of events like this happens, especially given that it involves people who never talked to each other or even met each other. The clear arrangement in these events speaks powerfully for the inspiration of scripture.

It also speaks powerfully for the priesthood of Jesus. He is not a Levitical priest. He is a priest according to a different and superior order—the order of Melchizedek.

Chapter 6: The widening circle of truth

The author of Hebrews begins his argument about Jesus and Melchizedek in chapter 5, but he goes on a lengthy digression about the apparent immaturity of his readers at the end of chapter 5 and the beginning of chapter 6 (and we will study that section in our next chapter). For now we continue following his argument about Melchizedek, beginning in 6:13:

> For when God made the promise to Abraham, since He could swear by no one greater, He swore by Himself, saying, "I will surely bless you and I will surely multiply you" ...For men swear by one greater than themselves, and with them an oath given as confirmation is an end of every dispute. In the same way God, desiring even more to show to the heirs of the promise the unchangeableness of His purpose, interposed with an oath, so that by two unchangeable things in which it is impossible for God to lie, we who have taken refuge would have strong encouragement to take hold of the hope set before us. (Hebrews 6:13-18)

Although this section may seem rather random, he is focusing on God's promise-making. When something is really important, God has been known to interpose with an oath for the sake of emphasis. Thus, when sealing the covenant with Abraham, God swore an ancient oath.

This account comes from Genesis 15, when God had Abraham divide some animal corpses, forming two lines with a path between. In normal ancient practice, the parties to a contract would link arms and walk between the corpses as a way of saying, "May God (or the gods) do this to me if I break this covenant."[15]

---

[15] You can see another reference to this practice in Jeremiah 34:18-20. For more information see theopedia.com/covenant.

The strange thing in Genesis 15 is that only God passed between the animals while promising things; Abraham just watched. Thus, in a sense, God was swearing by himself—he alone would keep the covenant—making the promise unconditional and unilateral. This is why our author says, "For when God made the promise to Abraham, since He could swear by no one greater, He swore by Himself" (v. 13). God can't swear by someone or something greater than himself, because no such thing exists. Therefore, swearing by himself is the ultimate level of assurance God can give when making a promise (see another example in Gen. 22:16).

This remarkable event in Genesis is similar to God's promise in Psalms 110. There we read that "The Lord has sworn and will not change his mind...." In this case, the promise is that King Messiah will also be a priest forever after the order of Melchizedek. So the point for his readers, and for us, is that we have a firm and infallible basis for our confidence that Jesus has taken over the high priesthood forever.

The very fact that God would frame the promise by swearing an oath signifies emphasis; God is telling us this is important. And that leads to the author's conclusion: "This hope we have as an anchor of the soul, a hope both sure and steadfast and one which enters within the veil, where Jesus has entered as a forerunner for us, having become a high priest forever according to the order of Melchizedek" (vs. 19-20).

Five More Observations on Melchizedek

Just as we noted several keys to the story of Melchizedek in the previous chapter, it turns out our author sees the same things (actually, I got these five points from him).

1. *Melchizedek's strange name and title*:

> For this Melchizedek, king of Salem, priest of the Most High God, who met Abraham as he was returning from the slaughter of the kings and blessed him... was first of all, by the translation of his name, king of righteousness, and then also king of Salem, which is king of peace. (Hebrews 7:1-2)

Our author sees that these titles are not accidental. The king of righteousness and peace must be a "type" (or symbol) of Christ.

2. *Melchizedek's lack of lineage or credentials for being great*: The author observes that Melchizedek is "without father, without mother, without genealogy" (v. 3). He isn't saying that Melchizedek didn't have parents, only that they aren't mentioned in the Genesis account. This is the unusual absence of any lineage we noted earlier.

3. *An eternal priest*: Then our author says, "Having neither beginning of days nor end of life, but made like the Son of God, he remains a priest perpetually" (v. 3). He is not referring here to the original Melchizedek in Genesis 14, but rather to Psalm 110:4. That is where we read "you are a priest forever." This passage predicts a version of Melchizedek that is eternal, namely the Messiah.

Some commentators think he is referring to the original Melchizedek, but we see nothing in the Genesis narrative that would point to his eternality. Teachers who believe this is referring to Genesis 14, usually also believe the man Melchizedek was actually an appearance by Jesus in his pre-incarnate form. But again, I think it's easier to read this as saying Melchizedek is a *type* of Christ, based on the authority of Psalm 110. The original Melchizedek was, according to the text, the king of an ancient city—an actual man who lived a life like others. This is inconceivable for the Son of God at that time, and it would be reading too much into the text of Genesis.

4. *Melchizedek is superior to Abraham, based on the giving of the tithe and the blessing*: Next our author explains how Abraham giving a tithe and receiving a blessing points to the supremacy of Melchizedek's priesthood over the Levitical priesthood. "Now observe how great this man was to whom Abraham, the patriarch, gave a tenth..." (v.4). There follows a difficult-to-read paragraph in 7:5-10. In this section, the author simply observes that because Abraham gave a tithe, and was blessed by Melchizedek, he was acknowledging Melchizedek as his priest and his superior, since "without any dispute the lesser is blessed by the greater" (v. 7). He also observes that the Levitical priests of a later century gave this

tithe as well in a sense, because they were children of Abraham. Therefore the Levitical priesthood also had to be subordinate to that of Melchizedek.

5. *Jesus coming from the tribe of Judah doesn't matter for his priesthood*: The author has anticipated objections about Jesus' tribal lineage:

> For the one concerning whom these things are spoken belongs to another tribe, from which no one has officiated at the altar. For it is evident that our Lord was descended from Judah, a tribe with reference to which Moses spoke nothing concerning priests. (Hebrews 7:13-14)

But he points out that Jesus didn't get his authorization to be a high priest from Moses or from being in the right tribe, but from direct divine authorization in Psalms 110.

> And this is clearer still, if another priest arises according to the likeness of Melchizedek, who has become such not on the basis of a law of physical requirement, but according to the power of an indestructible life. For it is attested of Him, "You are a priest forever according to the order of Melchizedek." (vs. 15-17)

Once God inspired this psalm, he rendered the whole question of tribes irrelevant. The priesthood of Melchizedek is a completely different paradigm, standing outside and above the Moses covenant.

What's the point?

So, Jesus is our high priest, and not one of the Old Testament Levitical priests, but in the loftier order of Melchizedek—and not temporarily, but permanently. But is this just fussing over obscure points, or is there something important here? Next we learn that this priesthood business is the tip of a very large iceberg.

Anticipation proves limitation

Jesus' priesthood sends out shockwaves that completely revolutionize everything in the Bible's message. Our author first asks,

> Now if perfection was through the Levitical priesthood (for on the basis of it the people received the Law), what further need was

there for another priest to arise according to the order of
Melchizedek, and not be designated according to the order of
Aaron? (v. 11)

Good point! If the covenant of Moses was the answer for all time, why
would God promise that a different kind of priest was coming in the person
of the Messiah? This prediction proves that God always viewed the Mosaic
covenant as temporary and not the final answer. Anyone clinging to the
Mosaic Covenant (like the readers of Hebrews) must be baffled at this
undeniable teaching on the priesthood of Melchizedek.

Contract changed

Then he says,

For when the priesthood is changed, of necessity there takes place a
change of law also. (v. 12)

It's not just the priesthood that God changed. Here the author observes that
you cannot change part of the Old Testament covenant without changing all
of it.

The Mosaic covenant is an agreement, or contract. The people agreed to
live by the law (see Exodus 24:3). God agreed to bless them if they did (c.f.
Deuteronomy 28). A second section in the covenant deals with what
happens if the people fall short of their obligations to obey the law of God.
This is the part where they bring their sin offerings to the temple and the
priests present it to God. This is also where holy days like the Day of
Atonement come in (Leviticus 16).

Now, if these are section A and section B in the Mosaic covenant, what
happens when we pick up the contract and tear off section B (because the
priesthood has changed)? Today, like then, you can't just tear off half a
contract and have the other half remain in force. When you tear off the
bottom half, *the entire contract becomes null and void*!

Now we see that Jesus' priesthood is not an add-on to the old covenant, but
that it completely replaces that covenant. This is not an exaggeration, but
the unmistakable message of Hebrews.

Complete and total exchange

This abrogation of the old covenant is absolute and total.

> For, on the one hand, there is a setting aside of a former
> commandment because of its weakness and uselessness (for the
> Law made nothing perfect), and on the other hand there is a
> bringing in of a better hope, through which we draw near to God.
> (Hebrews 7:18-19)

Here we have one of the most radical and revolutionary passages in the
Bible. When our author talks about a "setting aside" of the Law, he uses
strong language. To get an idea how *athetasis* and its parent verb, *atheteo*,
are used, consider Hebrews 9:26: "But now once at the consummation of
the ages He has been manifested to *put away* (*athetasin*) sin by the sacrifice
of Himself." *Atheteo* is translated in the New Testament as "reject," "bring
to nothing," "frustrate," "disannul," and "cast off." He is clearly not just
saying the Old Testament law has been demoted or lowered in importance.
Rather, it is *nullified* and *completely set aside*.

This comes as quite a shock to many modern readers, as it no doubt was to
the original readers. Can he really be saying that the covenant that includes
the law of Moses has been annulled? Commentators who believe Christians
are still under law line up to find ways to deny the clear import of these
verses.

Some have argued that only the ceremonial portion of the law is set aside.
But that's wrong. We just read that "when the priesthood is changed, of
necessity there takes place a change of law also" (Hebrews 7:12). The
priesthood is the ceremonial part, so "change of law" refers to something
else—the rest of the law.

Neither is he referring to discarding the law as a means for salvation. The
law never had that purpose or capability.[16] The passages before us show that

---

[16] Personal salvation never comes up in this passage. The Mosaic Covenant was never about how to be saved or
go to heaven. It was about establishing a nation that would lay the needed groundwork for the coming of Christ.
People in the Old Testament knew they were saved by faith, not by works or ceremony. This is why David can
say, "You do not desire a sacrifice, or I would offer one. You do not want a burnt offering. The sacrifice you
desire is a broken spirit. You will not reject a broken and repentant heart, O God" (Psalm 51:16-17). Moses wrote

something changed in our relationship to the law as a result of Jesus' life and work. What changed? Not that people used to be saved by works of law. The change is in the path to spiritual growth, not spiritual birth.

Some Christian teachers to this day are reluctant to accept the message of this passage, along with numerous others that teach the same thing. These teachers believe the law is good for spiritual growth. But they must answer the question of why the Bible would say the law is "weak and useless." What way is this to talk about a code that helps Christians grow? Isn't this statement just like Paul's equally radical claim that "sin shall not be master over you, for you are not under law but under grace" (Romans 6:14)?

Why discard the law? Because "the law made nothing perfect" or mature. The word *telios* means "complete," but can also be translated "perfect" or completed in the sense of someone who has had his deficiencies made good. See Hebrews 5:14 where we read, "Solid food is for the mature (*telios*)...." It's not that Christians are ever perfect in our sense of the word, as without any flaw, but some are mature.[17]

It is precisely in promoting spiritual growth that the law falls down and must be discarded. God's law has its purposes. It serves as "a tutor to lead us to Christ, so that we may be justified by faith" (Galatians 3:24). But don't miss the follow up: "But now that faith has come, we are no longer under a tutor" (v. 25). Paul explains, "Now we know that whatever the Law says, it speaks to those who are under the Law, so that every mouth may be closed and all the world may become accountable to God" (Romans 3:19). This is what the law does well. It convicts people of sin and shows them their need for forgiveness in Jesus.

The problem comes in when we think obeying the law is a good way to grow in the Lord. Exactly the opposite is true. Look at the next verse in Hebrews 7: "and on the other hand there is a bringing in of a better hope,

---

of Abraham's salvation saying "Abram believed the Lord, and the Lord counted him as righteous because of his faith" (Genesis 15:6; and see Paul's observations on the same passage in Romans 4:1-13).

[17] Or, consider Hebrews 5:9: "And having been made perfect, He became to all those who obey Him the source of eternal salvation." Here again, we know that Jesus was never made perfect in the sense that he was imperfect before. Rather, this verse is teaching that the requirements for his priestly role were completed through his suffering. So we see the author of Hebrews using the word this way, and that he is mainly concerned with his readers growing to maturity.

through which we draw near to God" (v. 19). This "on the one hand... on the other hand" language means these two actions are directly related. Before we can bring in the better hope and draw near to God, we must set aside the law.

This is exactly where the readers of Hebrews were going wrong. Their clinging to the law was causing distance from God resulting in atrophy in their spiritual lives. Still today, when Christians turn to the law the result is an external, superficial do-gooding that is an ugly parody of true spirituality. Real spirituality begins with drawing close to God through grace alone. That means the law must first be set aside.

Of course, we're not saying the law is gone in the sense that it is no longer a valid portrayal of God's character. The point is not that the law disappears, but that we are no longer *under it*. The law has been annulled when it comes to Christians. This is why Paul can say, "But now we have been released from the Law, having died to that by which we were bound, so that we serve in newness of the Spirit and not in oldness of the letter" (Romans 7:6).

Why an oath?

The shuddering impact of this passage on the readers must have been incredible, and no doubt our author sensed that. That's why he goes back to add further emphasis to his point.

> This new system was established with a solemn oath. Aaron's descendants became priests without such an oath, but there was an oath regarding Jesus. For God said to him, "The Lord has taken an oath and will not break his vow: 'You are a priest forever.'" Because of this oath, Jesus is the one who guarantees this better covenant with God. (Hebrews 7:20-22 NLT)

I've quoted the NLT here because it is easier to read and the point is more obvious. Our author is again stressing that when we read a phrase like that in Psalms 110:4—"The Lord has sworn and will not change his mind"—we are seeing emphatic language. By adding this kind of emphasis, God is stressing that he means it and that people should not ignore it or alter it through interpretive side-stepping.

Permanence versus replacement

In Hebrews 7:23-25 our author contrasts the fact that Old Testament priests had to pass the priesthood on to others, whereas Jesus is given his priesthood permanently. The theological implication is that since his priesthood is permanent, the salvation he gives is also permanent (v. 25). Unlike Old Testament priests, whose sacrifices pictured forgiveness only from one sacrifice to the next, "Jesus did this once for all when he offered himself as the sacrifice for the people's sins" (v. 27). This is the first mention in Hebrews of the "once for all" nature of Jesus' offering, but not the last. The once for all expression is a way of pointing to the finished work of Christ.

The big picture

By proving that Jesus is now our only valid priest, our author has proven that the entire edifice of ritual Judaism has no place in Christian or Jewish practice. But he has also proven that legalism has no place. Anyone who believes the Old Testament is inspired scripture must admit that this is not a later twisting by Christians, but is built into the message of the Old Testament itself. Thank God we are the privileged recipients of the new covenant with all its freedom and confident closeness with God!

The realization that we are truly no longer under law works a spiritual miracle in the hearts of grace-oriented believers. The constant worry and guilt so many believers feel dissipates. Instead of measuring our performance, we can turn our attention to experiencing the love of God as we draw close to him. The better our relationship gets, the more we will enjoy serving God and others out of his power instead of self-effort.

Chapter 7: Warning on the sin of failing to grow

Just as our author is working up to the full intensity of the Melchizedek saga, he intuitively senses that his audience is probably not understanding:

> Concerning him we have much to say, and it is hard to explain, since you have become dull of hearing. For though by this time you ought to be teachers, you have need again for someone to teach you the elementary principles of the oracles of God, and you have come to need milk and not solid food. (Hebrews 5:11-12)

These believers were spiritually sick. Any time we see Christians not progressing, we must feel confused. Why is this happening? What went wrong? For it is desperately wrong. Arrested spiritual growth can result from a number of causes.

At the worst extreme, it could signal that a person is not truly born again. Superficial believers, like the rocky soil in Jesus parable, "receive the word with joy" but "it has no root within them" and the plant dies (Matthew 13:20). This could be a case of one who feels attracted to the Christian community for social reasons, but has not inwardly surrendered to Jesus in true faith. Healthy spiritual growth is quite impossible for one who has never received the Holy Spirit.

Yet, absence of the Holy Spirit is only one possible reason for arrested growth. The author of Hebrews doesn't necessarily consider these immature readers non-Christian, although false conversion is one possibility. For most, their feebleness derives from problems within their Christian lives. This is clear in other New Testament books where we find immature and un-spiritually minded believers (e.g. 1 Corinthians 3:1-4).

Any believer who becomes too attached to a serious pattern of sin could derail his or her growth. Jesus warned that "the worries and cares of the world and the deceitfulness of riches" cause unfruitfulness. So too, anyone who fails to regularly partake in any one of the main means God has given us for growth (scripture, prayer, fellowship, serving love, and suffering in faith) will eventually see his or her growth arrested.

Legalism also arrests spiritual growth by diverting people's attention away from what leads to growth and toward rules that "are of no value against fleshly indulgence" (Colossians 2:23).

For the readers, our author mentions three contributing factors:

1. They have become "dull of hearing"

Being dull of hearing is not a condition people acquire like a disease or a handicap. Christians are dull of hearing because they want to be. Dull hearing describes an attitude problem—willful sloth and sullen unwillingness to really hear anything that challenges their sinful life.

Unless our lives are awakened to hunger for spiritual instruction, we cannot hear properly. Jesus explained that he spoke in hard-to-understand parables because "the heart of this people has become dull" (Matthew 13:15). He told his disciples, "To you it has been granted to know the mysteries of the kingdom of heaven, but to them [the multitude] it has not been granted" (Matthew 13:11). God does not prostitute his truth. When people stop listening from the heart, he stops speaking. Andrew Murray explains:

> The writer's complaint is not that they lack sufficient education or mental power to understand what he says. By no means. But spiritual things must be spiritually discerned. Spiritual truth can only be received by the spiritual mind, by a heart that thirsts for God, and sacrifices this world for the knowledge and enjoyment of the unseen One.[18]

In their negative attitude, probably stemming from their reluctance to go the rest of the way with Jesus, they were losing the ability to comprehend spiritual truth. This spiritual denseness is partly a subconscious way to avoid looking at something you don't want to look at, and it reinforces itself by making it truly difficult to see what is right in front of your face.

---

[18] Andrew Murray, *The Holiest of All*, 186.

2. *They are not accustomed to the word of righteousness*

Being "accustomed to the word of righteousness" means people study and learn God's word. Listening to rabbis or other teachers is not enough. Nothing can substitute for one's own time in learning and meditating on the Word of God. In ancient times, most people didn't have their own copies of the Bible like we do. Instead, they memorized large tracks of scripture during public readings, and could recite lengthy parts from Old Testament books.

We read that these same believers in their early days "continually devoted themselves to the apostles teaching" (Acts. 2:42). But our author is clear that things have deteriorated since those days, decades earlier.

Most of these readers were probably now second generation believers. About thirty years had passed since Acts 2, so most of the people in that original group were probably dead by now. Very often in Christian history, strong movements of the Holy Spirit have fizzled when the second or third generation fails to see what their parents saw. They continue going through the motions, but without the spiritual power the group had earlier.

When we don't use our spiritual knowledge, it gradually slips away, as Jesus warned when he said, "Whoever does not have, even what he has shall be taken away from him" (Matthew 13:12). What a scary thought! Our knowledge of God is dynamic. It's either growing or declining. When we don't sincerely take in the word and act on it, confusion and darkness replace what used to be so clear.

People in this condition may still comprehend the rudiments of the word, but they have become milk drinkers who cannot grasp the deeper truths and their significance. They fit the description in verse 13: "For everyone who partakes only of milk is not accustomed to the word of righteousness, for he is an infant." Receiving spiritual insight from God is a rare gift, and trifling with it could result in disaster. Dull hearing is a sin of omission, but this passage shows that omissive sin is just as serious as sins of commission.

3. They have not trained their senses through practice

Biblical truth is different than knowledge we get from reading a history or
science book. With scripture, we cannot fully understand the text until we
act on it in faith. Scripture does contain propositional truth, but there's
more. This spiritual word goes beyond naked propositions to call our hearts
in subjective and moral ways. The word calls us to account and exposes
deep need for change.

James warns about the consequences of being "forgetful hearers rather than
effectual doers." People who merely listen to God's word without acting on
it cannot grasp the text's significance. They also lose their passion for the
things of God. Too many Christians today, just as then, settle for
pontificating about God's word, when in fact their spiritual lives are
relatively dead. The resulting pronouncements are noticeably dead and ring
hollow.

Faith is essential to a true understanding of scripture, and faith is only
adequate when we believe the word enough to act on it. Then, when we see
God come through, we realize how true his word really is, and our faith
grows even more. The Holy Spirit uses our action to deepen our wisdom.
We "have our senses trained to discern good and evil" (v. 14). God blesses
practitioners of the word with living insight that mere theoreticians never
know. For such practitioners, God fulfills verse 14: "But solid food is for
the mature."

The big picture

Keeping our hearing sensitive to God, reading and meditating on his word,
and believing enough to act in accordance with what we read—these are the
makings of spiritual maturity. The compromised readers of Hebrews were
falling short in all three areas. No wonder our author imagines them staring
slack-jawed and uncomprehending at his advanced discussion about the
priesthood of Melchizedek.

Chapter 8: Correcting the problem

When calling his readers away from their malaise, the author presses straight ahead in a way that shows this chapter division is one of the most awkward and strange in the New Testament (remember, these divisions were introduced centuries later). His thought is ongoing, as seen from the first word, "therefore":

> Therefore leaving the elementary teaching about the Christ, let us press on to maturity, not laying again a foundation of repentance from dead works and of faith toward God, of instruction about washings and laying on of hands, and the resurrection of the dead and eternal judgment. And this we will do, if God permits. (Hebrews 6:1-3)

Observing this section, F. F. Bruce says, "It is remarkable how little in the list is distinctive of Christianity, for practically every item could have its place in a fairly orthodox Jewish community."[19] This is an important point missed by many Christian readers.

When we read "teaching about the Christ," we might think he means teaching about Jesus, and that's possible. But remember, pre-Christian Jews also taught about the Messiah. Of course their views were "elementary" and missed so much that came to light during Jesus' life. The rabbis had completely missed, for instance, the true significance of teachings like the priesthood of Melchizedek. "Repentance from dead works" would have been a standard part of any synagogue teaching, as was "faith toward God."

The phrase "instructions about washings" probably refers to the ritual washings that had come to play a big part in Judaism during this period (see Mark 7:1-23). It is not referring to Christian water baptism, because the plural here (baptisms, or washings, not baptism) points away from the Christian view that there is only one baptism (Ephesians 4:5). NIV is

---

[19] F. F. Bruce, *The Epistle to the Hebrews*, in *New International Commentary on the New Testament* (Grand Rapids: Wm. B. Eerdmans Publishing Co.) 138.

correct to translate "instruction about cleansing rites." Because this item is definitely *not* referring to Christian teaching it strongly suggests the rest of the list refers to pre-Christian Jewish teaching as well. Why would the author insert a Jewish-only teaching topic into a list of Christian topics?

"Laying on of hands" probably refers to attempts to heal or bless, both of which were common in Judaism. "The resurrection of the dead and eternal judgment" were also central themes in conservative Judaism, just as they are in Christian teaching.

So what's going on here?

We've seen that the readers acknowledged Jesus on some level, but apparently didn't fully grasp the extent of his person and work. They probably went over some of his teaching, but must have spent a lot of time in their meetings continuing to analyze the Old Testament much as they always had. They were stuck trying to synchronize rabbinic views of the Old Testament with Jesus' teaching. This traditional approach was one of the key reasons they weren't growing in insight. Under such muddled teaching, even continuing to access the temple could be justified, or at least tolerated. This leads to the dire warning:

> For in the case of those who have once been enlightened and have tasted of the heavenly gift and have been made partakers of the Holy Spirit, and have tasted the good word of God and the powers of the age to come, and then have fallen away, it is impossible to renew them again to repentance, since they again crucify to themselves the Son of God and put Him to open shame. (Hebrews 6:4-6)

This ominous passage seems very menacing at first reading, possibly teaching that falling away from Jesus is a one-way ticket to hell with no possible reprieve. Or is it not that? Perhaps it's teaching nothing more than what the author of Hebrews has argued all along–that continuing in ritual Judaism is incompatible with following Jesus. A third possible reading is that this passage is about pseudo-Christians. Such false believers are mixed in with real Christians for a time, but come to light when they walk away from God.

To help arbitrate this debate let's notice four points:

1. The people described in verses 4 and 5 might not be true believers. Commentators notice guarded language here that seems ambiguous. To "once be enlightened" refers to receiving revelation, but not necessarily to believing it. To "taste" of the word of God and the powers of the age to come (witnessing miracles?) is different than drinking deeply. Perhaps someone who shows up for fellowship, hears teaching, and even sees prayers answered would fit this description even if he or she didn't truly believe.

2. The strongest phrase is that they "have been made partakers of the Holy Spirit." Some point out that this isn't the unmistakable expression "sealed with the Spirit," but a more ambiguous word meaning "partner" or "one who shares in." Under this view, these could be people who "rub shoulders" with the Holy Spirit by being in the presence of his working, but never really surrender to Jesus. The problem with this reading is that the author uses the same expression in 3:14 to refer to true Christians (unless the verse in chapter 3 is referring to being partners with God in his mission for the world rather than conversion).

3. What does it mean that these people might "fall away?" The word has a wide range of meaning, all related to the idea of falling down or erring. In this passage, it must be linked to the last phrase, which charges the same people with "again crucifying to themselves the Son of God, and putting him to open shame." In the context of Hebrews, this is almost undoubtedly referring to people returning to the Old Testament sacrificial system. To offer an animal sacrifice when Jesus already fulfilled our need for sacrifice is an insult! By acting like Jesus' sacrifice wasn't enough, they might as well be nailing Jesus to the cross again. It exposes him to open shame—the shame of having failed to complete his work the first time. This verse clearly shows that

some in the Jewish Christian church in question have departed from a dependence on grace and have returned to Old Testament religion. Later in the book, it appears many of them no longer even attend Christian fellowship (10:25).

4.   Why would the author say that "it is impossible to renew them again to repentance?" (v. 6). The answer is tied up with how the two phrases in the proposition are linked—whether they are causal or conditional. Notice how the NASB gives a marginal alternative: "It is impossible... *while* they again crucify" instead of "*since* they again crucify." That is a possible translation for this expression, and how different it is from the alternative!

According to one reading, it is impossible to restore certain kinds of people to repentance, apparently because they have gone too far for that. Under the other reading, they cannot be restored to repentance until and unless they give up their insulting practices at the temple.

The second reading would fit the argument of Hebrews perfectly: that returning to ritual Judaism is incompatible with following Jesus. The other reading is not unprecedented in the New Testament (i.e. that there is a point of no return in refusing Jesus; see Matthew 12:32) but seems to fly in from left field here. How would the author know that these people have blasphemed the Spirit or are irretrievably lost? And what is he saying to the others? Just forget about them; they're all going to hell?

This latter reading seems very improbable to me, and really no more suited to the Greek than the other reading. From the perspective of context, it seems far more reasonable to say that they cannot be restored *until* they admit they are in the wrong and quit offering sacrifice.[20]

---

[20] My reading here is in the minority. Most commentators prefer the reading "since" or "because" (although neither word is in the Greek text, but must be inferred as the link to the last phrase). Then they interpret accordingly, depending on their starting point. Interpreters who believe in eternal security for Christians argue

So which is right?

Considering these observations, we can return to the debate mentioned above: is this passage referring to people losing their salvation? Or to people who never had true salvation? Or, taking verse 6 as above, could these be believers still who simply cannot have their lives set right with God as long as they continue in their unbelieving practices? Under this last reading, repentance would mean the need to turn away from a sinful reliance on ritual and works.

On one level, this is an academic question that matters little. When people walk away from God, is it because they lost their salvation, or because they never had it? Or are they like the prodigal son, who was a son the whole time he lived in the distant country? In most cases, we don't know.

In my opinion, the view that people lose their salvation has too many problems to be sustained in light of the overall scope of biblical teaching (including Hebrews, which contains strong verses on security, like 7:25). But many Bible-believing people think losing one's salvation is possible.

Whether or not they are true believers, this passage is mainly warning that those who accommodate or return to ritual Judaism cannot be right with God until that changes.

When you think about it, the author has no way to know what their inner state is. This passage describes a class of people, not an individual, so that makes it even more impossible to know the inner lives of all the individuals involved. He probably wrote this in a way that could fit either possibility. The author knew people were defecting. Were they true believers, or pseudo-believers? Only God could know. The point in this section (and the whole book) is that there is no middle ground between reliance on grace and reliance on works. When people abandon complete trust in the finished

---

that these are pseudo-Christians who have now proven their falsity by defecting. Radical Arminian interpreters see this as a plain warning that Christians can and do lose their salvation. Neither school adequately explains the one-way language. Why would falling away be irreversible? Why would being a pseudo-Christian be irreversible? This is the key question. Once we see that it is not irreversible—only that it cannot be reversed *until they leave off their apostate practices* with ritual legalism—the passage is no longer a problem. It doesn't matter whether they are true Christians or not. The statement would fit either way.

work of Christ, they fall immediately and completely into disastrous law living.

A qualification

Our author quickly moves to a more positive note for most of his readers: "But, beloved, we are convinced of better things concerning you, and things that accompany salvation, though we are speaking in this way" (v. 9).[21] He no doubt realizes that most of them haven't reached that level of apostasy yet, and, he may hope that being positive will be more motivating than being negative.

When he refers to their "work and the love which you have shown toward His name, in having ministered and in still ministering to the saints" (v. 10), it again shows that this used to be a strong group. At some point in the past they must have been awesome. Even now, some are still serving. This scenario fits the Jerusalem church. His reference to God not forgetting their earlier service refers to God's relationship with them, not to repaying their works.

NASB is hard to follow in verse 11 and 12, but NLT is much easier:

> Our great desire is that you will keep on loving others as long as life lasts, in order to make certain that what you hope for will come true. Then you will not become spiritually dull and indifferent. Instead, you will follow the example of those who are going to inherit God's promises because of their faith and endurance.

The author administered his warning but followed it with this alternative. If they return to faith, the future looks bright. The dullness that afflicts them could change quickly. Notice, we have come full circle in vs. 11-12 when he points out that the "full assurance" that grace provides will keep them from being "dull and indifferent." This is what he's worried about—not that they will end up in hell, but that their dullness will increase and hold them

---

[21] His contrast between what he has been saying and "things that belong to salvation" could imply that he sees the defectors in v. 9 as non-Christians. However, the term "salvation" is often used in the New Testament of spiritual growth or healing, so we can't be sure.

back from the blessings they should be experiencing in a close walk with
God.

The big picture

The Jerusalem church may never have fully grasped the implications that
the gospel of grace holds for traditional Judaism. James pointed out to Paul
how the thousands of believers in Jerusalem were "all zealous for the Law"
(Acts 21:20-21). Perhaps because of this clinging to the old way, people's
theology became increasingly confused. Even as early as the Jerusalem
council in Acts 15 a significant minority opposed Paul's abandonment of
circumcision and the law. This might have been one of the reasons the
epicenter of Christian mission seems to shift away from Jerusalem to
Antioch.

Chapter 9: Call Jeremiah

In the chapters that follow the discussion on Melchizedek, our author presses the point, showing other, parallel arguments for abandoning the old covenant. At the heart of most of these arguments is the idea that when comparing Old and new covenants, the superiority of the new strongly suggests that the old should be discarded.

Sinful priests

At the end of chapter 7 he says,

> For it was fitting for us to have such a high priest, holy, innocent, undefiled, separated from sinners and exalted above the heavens; who does not need daily, like those high priests, to offer up sacrifices, first for His own sins and then for the sins of the people, because this He did once for all when He offered up Himself. For the Law appoints men as high priests who are weak, but the word of the oath, which came after the Law, appoints a Son, made perfect forever. (vs. 26-28)

Here, he points out that Old Testament priests were sinners themselves, so they had to first undergo a purifying ceremony before they could intercede. Jesus, on the other hand, had no need for this two-stage approach to God. He completed his work in one step at the cross. That's a superior priest.

Earthly versus heavenly

Chapter 8 continues the comparison. Here the author reveals that Jesus' offering of himself occurred not in the earthly temple, but in the heavenly sanctuary. It turns out that the tabernacle and the temple were both templates, imitating the real courtroom of God in heaven.

> Now the main point in what has been said is this: we have such a high priest, who has taken His seat at the right hand of the throne

> of the Majesty in the heavens, a minister in the sanctuary and in
> the true tabernacle, which the Lord pitched, not man. (vs. 1-2)

The tabernacle portrayed to humans how things are in heaven. The
enactment of substitutionary death and atonement in the tabernacle were
like a spiritual play. Plays imitate life, but the stories they tell are not real.
Even when plays are based on actual events, the play itself is not the event.
So too with tabernacle ritual. The author goes on to refer to Old Testament
priests:

> There are those who offer the gifts according to the Law; who
> serve as a copy and shadow of the heavenly things, just as Moses
> was warned by God when he was about to erect the tabernacle;
> for, "See," He says, "that you make all things according to the
> pattern which was shown you on the mountain." (Hebrews 8:4b-5,
> quoting Exodus 25:40)

Here is another reason why the tabernacle had to be made to such specific
dimensions and materials. Moses was creating a picture of how things work
in heaven, so God specified exactly how it should look and how it should be
used.

Calling Jeremiah to the witness stand

Priesthood wasn't the only reason for abandoning the old covenant. Our
author goes on to remind them that the Old Testament itself taught in the
book of Jeremiah that Moses' covenant was only temporary:

> For if there had been nothing wrong with that first covenant, no
> place would have been sought for another. But God found fault
> with the people and said: "The days are coming, declares the Lord,
> when I will make a new covenant with the house of Israel and with
> the house of Judah. It will not be like the covenant I made with
> their ancestors when I took them by the hand to lead them out of
> Egypt, because they did not remain faithful to my covenant, and I
> turned away from them, declares the Lord.
>
> This is the covenant I will establish with the house of Israel after
> that time, declares the Lord. I will put my laws in their minds and

write them on their hearts. I will be their God, and they will be my people. No longer will they teach their neighbors, or say to one another, 'Know the Lord,' because they will all know me, from the least of them to the greatest. For I will forgive their wickedness and will remember their sins no more." By calling this covenant "new," he has made the first one obsolete; and what is obsolete and outdated will soon disappear. (Hebrews 8:7-13)

In this thirty-first chapter of Jeremiah, God undeniably declares that the Mosaic Covenant is only temporary. He clearly promises that the new covenant "will not be like the covenant I made with their ancestors when I took them by the hand to lead them out of Egypt" (v. 9).

Facing the difference

The clear language here states that this new covenant is going to be very different from the old one, yet, most commentators today refuse to accept this difference. Walter Kaiser says, "When Paul referred to the law of Christ, he meant the Mosaic Law, which was also Jeremiah's new covenant law."[22] He thinks, "the new covenant should be called a 'renewed covenant,' that is, a renewed form of the Mosaic Law."[23] Similarly, Gerhard Von Rad argues that "the Mosaic Law still stands in the center of the new covenant. Jeremiah never announced that God's revelation given at Sinai would be nullified in whole or part."[24] If these statements are right, why does our author say the covenant is *not* like the one with Moses? I agree to the contrary with Adeyemi: "The phrase 'not like the covenant' in Jeremiah 31:32 is an absolute emphatic negation… This phrase does not suggest a mere renewal of the Mosaic Covenant."[25]

Paul certainly doesn't agree with the view that the two covenants are more or less similar, let alone the same:

---

[22] Walter Kaiser, "The Law as God's Gracious Guidance for the Promotion of Holiness," in *Five Views on Law and Gospel*, 189, 304. This view goes back to John Calvin in Protestant theology, (John Calvin, Commentaries on Jeremiah and Lamentations, 4:131-32) but is also in harmony with Catholic and Orthodox theology.

[23] Walter Kaiser, *The Uses of the Old Testament in the New*, 147-48.

[24] Gerhard von Rad, *Old Testament Theology*, 213.

[25] Femi Adeyemi, "What Is the New Covenant 'Law' in Jeremiah 31:33?" *Bibioteca Sacra*, 163:651 (Jul 2006)

> God made us adequate as servants of a new covenant, not of the
> letter but of the Spirit; for the letter kills, but the Spirit gives life...
> the ministry of death, in letters engraved on stones, came with
> glory. (2 Corinthians 3:6)

He is unmistakably referring to the Mosaic law with the expression "letters
engraved on stones." Nothing in the Old Testament other than the ten
commandments fits that description. You can also see from his language
that Paul considers the new covenant of the Spirit to be completely different
from the Mosaic law. He calls the old covenant "the ministry of death."
Again, such a negative description clearly points to the inadequacy of an
external legal code. The contrast between life and death couldn't be any
stronger.

External or internal?

This new covenant points to a new, higher level of spirituality possible with
the indwelling Holy Spirit, because God says "I will put my laws in their
minds and write them on their hearts" (v. 10). We don't relate to God on the
basis of an external code of rules.

Imagine me writing out a detailed list of agreed rules to be followed
between my wife and I. Then, when she comes and asks me to do
something, I pull out the list and scan down it. "Sorry, it's not on the list."
What is wrong with this picture? The fact is, we don't need a list of
obligations. Because of our relationship, I intuitively know what would
please my wife as she also would. In a close, personal relationship, turning
to an external code would be unnecessary and exceedingly strange—
suggesting distance rather than closeness.

Difference on forgiveness

The new covenant also points to pure grace when God says, "I will forgive
their wickedness and will remember their sins no more" (v. 12). Unlike the
old covenant, which is loaded with provisions for obtaining forgiveness for
sin (e.g. Leviticus 1-7), the new covenant sees no need for atoning acts,
because all our sins are forgiven the moment we receive Christ (Hebrews
10:14).

Partial fulfillment

Other aspects of this promised covenant have not been fulfilled. He says, "No longer will they teach their neighbors, or say to one another, 'Know the Lord,' because they will all know me, from the least of them to the greatest" (v. 11). This is not a good description of our world. We must continue to plead with people to know the Lord.

Some interpreters think Jeremiah's passage is now as fulfilled as it ever will be. Under this reading, the portions like verse 12 are "spiritualized"—that is, they won't be literally fulfilled. Others, including myself, think the complete fulfillment awaits Jesus' second coming. In the meantime, we have a partial fulfillment, where we partake in a real but not complete way in the promises of the future kingdom.[26] Either way, the point here in Hebrews is that the prophecy clearly teaches that the Mosaic Covenant will be superseded. That flies directly in the face of traditionalists who thought the old covenant was permanent. And so, the author's radical conclusion follows: "When He said, 'A new covenant,' He has made the first obsolete. But whatever is becoming obsolete and growing old is ready to disappear" (v. 13).

An ongoing problem

With such a clear prediction from Jeremiah that God was planning to move away from the old covenant and the laws, you would think that New Testament believers would be all over this promise. But that wasn't the case. These readers were compromised, trying to find some middle ground where they could keep part of the old.

Returning to God's covenant with Moses in whole or in part has continued to be a major problem throughout church history, and still today. People worry about what will happen if people come to believe they are no longer under law. They might go crazy! Actually, this is not the effect grace teaching has on people. To the contrary, grace is highly motivating for

---

[26] Other features in the same context in Jeremiah are also unfulfilled, such as, "'Behold, days are coming,' declares the Lord, 'when the city will be rebuilt for the Lord... it [Jerusalem] will not be plucked up or overthrown anymore forever'" (Jeremiah 31: 38, 40). This part has clearly not been fulfilled either literally or spiritually, but it will be after Jesus' second coming.

spiritual growth and doing good. While people may use God's grace as a license, that probably just shows they never truly grasped grace. In any case, it's a risk God is willing to take. The key here is not what will make people behave better, but what God declares in his word.

Bad fruit

Preaching law with its threatening only results in external compliance and internal distance from God. Christians under this kind of teaching generally end up faking it and exhibiting all the negative features that accompany legalism.

- They begin to "strain out the gnat while swallowing the camel"— overturning biblical priorities in ethics and making a huge fuss over relatively unimportant things (e.g. Matthew 23:24).

- They turn to formalism because they feel nervous about personal relating to a God they know is on a different level morally. Formalism, with its focus on ritual, feels safer than direct, close relating to legalistic believers.

- Hypocrisy is unavoidable. Only grace-based Christians can be truly honest about their lives.

- Non-Christians are not attracted to God like they are when Christians are under grace. Legalistic churches becomes ingrown and only win transfers from other churches.

- The ability to love others as Jesus wants us to requires grace. In a community based on grace, people feel safe opening up, they are able to forgive, and they draw closer to each other. None of these things happen under legalism.

Even if you are in a grace-based church, the danger of going under law is always close at hand. Individuals drift and lose their former love of grace. We need God to periodically open our eyes to grace in order to avoid drifting back into legalism.

How do legalistic teachers explain Jeremiah's clear statement about the shift away from law to grace, and the author of Hebrews' confirmation that it applies to us? They usually just focus on the issue of justification, or initial salvation by grace, but ignore the other part—that God has moved away from an external code engraved on stones to writing his law on our minds and hearts. Most Protestant Christian interpreters agree that salvation is by grace, but the law slips back in when it comes to spiritual growth.[27] But as we saw earlier, God never allowed people to be rescued through obedience to law (even in Old Testament times), so this explanation is missing the whole point. Our author isn't arguing that his readers need to forget about justification by law. He is arguing that they need to forget spiritual growth through law living.

---

[27] I discuss the question of law and spiritual growth more fully in *Walking in Victory: Why God's love can change your life like legalism never could*, (Columbus, OH: New Paradigm Publishing, 2012).

Chapter 10: Jesus and Old Testament ritual

To fully appreciate Jesus' work and God's plan of the ages, careful study of the Old Testament is essential. Jesus didn't just appear out of nowhere. If he had, nobody would have had any reason to believe him. Instead, he was fully prefigured, predicted, and set up for centuries before his coming. This was all according to God's careful, meticulous plan of rescue for humanity.

Jesus often pointed out that his life fulfilled predictive prophecy.

> Now He said to them, "These are My words which I spoke to you while I was still with you, that all things which are written about Me in the Law of Moses and the Prophets and the Psalms must be fulfilled." Then He opened their minds to understand the Scriptures. (Luke 24:44-45)

Clearly some psalms are Messianic, and the prophets gave us many direct predictions. But what did Moses write about Jesus? Actually, quite a bit—more than any other author! His material was a different kind of prediction called *typology*. Aside from festivals like Passover, a very large collection of types is associated with the tabernacle, which was Moses' forerunner to the temple.

The typology of the tabernacle involved a number of symbolic, divine dramas acting out principles involving God's holiness, sin, and atonement. Since most Israelites were illiterate and written materials far too expensive to supply to individual families, these visual enactments were a perfect way to get key spiritual themes across.

This was also important to our author's Jewish audience. If the author is saying they shouldn't be going to the temple anymore, why are these things taught and prescribed in the Bible? In the next two chapters of Hebrews we have the Bible's most complete explanation of the true meaning of the ritual system God prescribed to Moses.[28]

The Tabernacle

Our author begins his discussion with the tabernacle.

> Now even the first covenant had regulations of divine worship and the earthly sanctuary. For there was a tabernacle prepared, the outer one, in which were the lampstand and the table and the sacred bread; this is called the holy place. Behind the second veil there was a tabernacle which is called the Holy of Holies. (Hebrews 9:1-3)

Around the tabernacle itself was a sidewall made from animal hides and poles. This enclosure was the courtyard, not mentioned here. Only believing Jews could enter the courtyard, so it stood for the distinction between the people of God and the world.

The tabernacle itself was also called the "tent of meeting," not because people came there to have meetings, but because the tabernacle stood for a place where the people could meet God. It was a rectangular space made out of ten linen sheets draped around a wood structure. Over the top was a goat hair covering, and additional covering over that made of hides.

It wasn't very big—only about 45 feet long and a very narrow 12 feet wide. They didn't need much space because it wasn't anything like modern churches, where the whole congregation goes into the "sanctuary" and sits. With the tabernacle, the people stayed outside in the courtyard; only the priests went inside. The inside of the tabernacle was further divided into a

---

[28] Again, there is no essential difference between the functions of the tabernacle and the temple. The tabernacle was a movable tent for use during the Jews' wanderings in the wilderness. Later, Solomon built a permanent stone and wood temple in Jerusalem. That temple was destroyed by the Babylonians and later rebuilt during the time of Ezra and Nehemiah. This rebuilt temple was the one Jesus went to and was still standing when Hebrews was written. Naturally, the author refers to the tabernacle because that came first, and all the biblical legislation for ritual comes from passages about the tabernacle, not the temple. Worshippers at the later temple simply followed the earlier teaching on the tabernacle. To argue, as some do, that such references to the tabernacle means that Hebrews was written after the temple's destruction is unwarranted. The Old Testament had no other teaching on ritual to which he could have referred.

smaller area at one end a third of the total length, called the Holy of Holies (v. 3).

He also describes some of the furniture and symbolic objects found in the outer section, called the holy place. These stood for spiritual principles common to both the Old and New Testaments.

One was a table with what he calls "the sacred bread"—twelve loaves of bread, baked fresh each week. The loaves stood for the twelve tribes of Israel, and pictured their offering of themselves to God, just like we are called to do in Romans 12:1: "Therefore I urge you, brethren, by the mercies of God, to present your bodies a living and holy sacrifice, acceptable to God, which is your spiritual service of worship."

He also mentions the lampstand. You may have seen a menorah before— the seven-branched lampstand used to light the area (Exodus 25:31-39). A small oil lamp would be placed at the end of each branch. The lampstand stood for light, referring to God's enlightenment. Jesus explained that same light should spread through his people to the world (compare John 8:12 with Matthew 5:14-15).

One important piece not mentioned here in Hebrews is the so-called "brazen altar," probably because it was outside in the courtyard. This large altar was where most sacrifice took place. It had a big fire burning in it that could consume animals completely.

The Holy of Holies

Then came the inner sanctum called the Holy of Holies. This room stood symbolically for the actual throne room of God. People were not allowed into this area, not even priests. The author of Hebrews says the golden altar of incense was in this room, but that was only true part of the time. Incense produced smoke that ascended, and therefore symbolized the prayers of God's people ascending to God.

The other piece he explains in verses 4 and 5:

> ...the ark of the covenant covered on all sides with gold, in which
> was a golden jar holding the manna, and Aaron's rod which

budded, and the tables of the covenant; and above it were the
cherubim of glory overshadowing the mercy seat.

The word ark means a box, and that's what it was. It was made of wood and
plated with gold. Sometimes it was called the ark of the covenant, and other
times the ark of testimony. Both terms were appropriate because of the
contents of the box and how it was used in ancient worship.

The contents of the ark

Our author identifies three symbolic objects inside the ark.

Jar of manna

First he explains that the ark held a golden jar of manna. Manna was the
supernatural provision of food God made for the people of Israel during
their wanderings in the desolate Sinai peninsula. With no possibility of
farming or even large scale herding, the people were completely dependent
on God for food. He provided a white substance that would appear on the
ground each morning. People went out to gather it and used it like grain to
make flour and cakes (Numbers 11:7-8).

God explained the spiritual significance of manna in Deuteronomy 8:

Remember how the Lord your God led you all the way in the
desert these forty years… feeding you with manna, which neither
you nor your fathers had known, to teach you that man does not
live on bread alone but on every word that comes from the mouth
of the Lord. (vs. 2-3)

So manna was God's provision, and therefore parallel to his word—"every
word that comes from the mouth of the Lord." God's word is our provision
for survival and growth as well.

In the story of the wanderings, we read that the people got tired of manna.
In spite of the fact that eating manna was healthy, we read that the people
broke out with a rather irrational complaint:

The people spoke against God and Moses, "Why have you brought
us up out of Egypt to die in the wilderness? For there is no food
and no water, and we loathe this miserable food." (Numbers 21:5)

The miserable food they referred to was manna. This was the occasion when God sent serpents in as an act of discipline, and many died. So, manna not only stood for God's provision, it also stood for the people's rejection of that provision. In Exodus 16 we read, "As the Lord commanded Moses, so Aaron placed it [a jar of manna] before the Testimony, to be kept" (v. 34).

Aaron's rod which budded

Aaron's walking stick grew buds and leaves in an incident recorded in Numbers 16-17. A group of tribal leaders came before Moses, announcing that he had gone far enough, and they had decided to take over leadership. Readers of Exodus know that Moses' leadership was not a matter of human decision making. God himself had called Moses to lead the people and had backed his leadership at every point. These men had no right to depose Moses.

In response to this revolt, God told each leader and Aaron (standing in for Moses) to write their names on their walking sticks and put them in the tabernacle over night. The next day we read, "Moses went into the tent of the testimony; and behold, the rod of Aaron for the house of Levi had sprouted and put forth buds and produced blossoms, and it bore ripe almonds" (Numbers 17:8). This was a clear statement that God would not allow any change in leadership.

Having validated Moses' authority, God moved to discipline the rebels. But we also read in verse 10, "The Lord said to Moses, 'Put back the rod of Aaron before the testimony to be kept as a sign against the rebels.'" So the second object in the ark of testimony was this stick that symbolized God's authority and humanity's rebellion against that authority.

The tablets of the covenant

The third symbol in the ark was the two tablets of the law. These were the stone tablets (probably far smaller than in the movies) containing the ten commandments, said to be written by the actual finger of God.

Of course, those familiar with the story will remember that these laws were being broken by the people at the base of the mountain as fast as God could write them. Moses came down from Mount Sinai to find a wild polytheistic party in progress, and he threw the tablets in anger (Exodus 32:19). Later God had Moses go back up the mountain and get replacement tablets for the broken ones. This time Moses recounts, "I put the tablets in the ark which I had made; and there they are, as the Lord commanded me" (Deuteronomy 10:5).

The mercy seat

Reading on, Hebrews 9 explains,

> Above the Ark were the cherubim of divine glory, whose wings stretched out over the Ark's cover, the place of atonement. But we cannot explain these things in detail now. (v. 5 NLT)

Unlike the sides and bottom of the ark, which were made of gold-plated wood, the lid was a solid plate of cast gold. At each end of the plate they fashioned two angels, called cherubim. In Exodus 25 God gave detailed instructions for building this part of the ark:

> Then make two cherubim from hammered gold, and place them on the two ends of the atonement cover. Mold the cherubim on each end of the atonement cover, making it all of one piece of gold. The cherubim will face each other and look down on the atonement cover with their wings spread above it. (vs. 18-20 NLT)

These angelic beings, called cherubs, were fashioned to have their wings spread over the solid gold lid of the ark, but they were also to have their heads turned downward so their gaze was toward the so-called mercy seat. Symbolically, then, they were looking straight through the plate onto the symbolic contents of the ark below.

The stage is set

Now the ark was ready to play its part in the drama of atonement. The author of Hebrews explains:

> When these things were all in place, the priests regularly entered the first room as they performed their religious duties. But only the high priest ever entered the Most Holy Place, and only once a

> year. And he always offered blood for his own sins and for the sins
> the people had committed in ignorance. (Hebrews 9:6-7)

"The first room" here refers to the outer part of the tabernacle, the holy place. That area was in constant, daily use. But the inner part, the Holy of Holies, only came into play once a year on *Yom Kippur*, the day of atonement.

Between these two areas hung a cloth veil. This veil was the drop-dead line between God and humans. In the tabernacle, people could approach God through the priests and the rituals, but only so far. They had to stay a certain distance from God, and this veil reminded them that God was too holy for profane, sinful humans to waltz into his presence.

One time, two sons of the high priest, Aaron, decided to go into the Holy of Holies on their own. Because their self-made ritual had not been prescribed by God, God called it "strange fire." The experiment didn't last long. We read, "Fire came out from the presence of the Lord and consumed them, and they died before the Lord" (Leviticus 10:2). God would not tolerate people trivializing his presence, and the boundary between him and sinful people could not be violated.

Only the high priest could enter the Holy of Holies, and only on this one special day each year—the day of atonement. When he pulled the veil aside and walked in, he carried in his hand a bowl containing blood from an animal sacrifice.

Blood was a symbol of life, as God explained in Leviticus 17:11:

> "For the life of the flesh is in the blood, and I have given it to you
> on the altar to make atonement for your souls; for it is the blood by
> reason of the life that makes atonement."

From the earliest part of the Bible, God had warned Adam, "In the day you eat of it [the forbidden fruit] you will surely die." Or, as Paul puts it, "the wages of sin is death." Since death is the sentence for sin, God chose blood as a symbol of that penalty. Farmers were well aware that as an animal bled, its life ebbed away. If your blood is on the ground, instead of in your body, you're dead.

Indeed an animal had died and contributed blood to the bowl in the high priest's hand. Now, as he approached the ark of testimony, he saw the picture described above. The cherubim, who could symbolize the whole population of the universe, looked on at the dilemma created by sin. Staring down into the ark, they saw God's moral will and humanity's violation of it (the tablets). They saw God's authority and human revolution against that authority (Aaron's rod). And they saw how God provided for human need and humans' rejection of his provision (the jar of manna).

Surely, this picture calls for action! We could imagine the heavenly hosts crying out, "God, you can't let this stand; you have to do something about this!" God might love humans, but if he looks the other way in the face of such rampant sin, he would contradict his own nature as righteous and fair.

Now, at the climactic moment, their gaze is suddenly blocked by blood as the priest uses his finger to sprinkle blood all over the mercy seat. The picture is complete. Now we can imagine the heavenly hosts seeing the blood: "Oh my, he did it! He let them have it. The sentence of death has been carried out."

Atonement. The word means satisfaction, and in this context God's justice is satisfied because the full sentence of death has been carried out. Of course, it isn't the guilty ones themselves who paid the price, but an innocent substitute.

But an animal could never truly substitute for a human. After all, animals are not even moral beings. Our author explains, "For it is impossible for the blood of bulls and goats to take away sins" (Hebrews 10:4).

Neither could a mere human be an adequate substitute. Any human would have his or her own sins to pay for. But even if a human were without sin, such a person could only reasonably substitute for one other human. Nothing but an infinite, perfect human could substitute for everyone. It had to be Jesus. And thus, we can finish Paul's thought: "The wages of sin is death, but the free gift of God is eternal life in Christ Jesus" (Romans 6:23).

When Jesus hung on the cross he cried out, "It is finished!" (John 19:30). This cry, which carries the idea of completion and full payment, was the last thing he said. We read that at that very moment, "The veil of the temple was torn in two from top to bottom" (Matthew 27:51). What an awesome statement from God! Instead of the veil blocking people's access to the presence of God, it was torn wide open. God made clear that the distance between him and us is no longer necessary. Now we can enter directly into the presence of God.

How perfectly and elegantly the work of Jesus was prefigured in the tabernacle worship! This particular section of Old Testament worship typology is amazing, but the other parts are just as good.

Anyone who fairly studies the whole Bible will be amazed to see how utterly integrated its single story line is. It is truly one book with this incredible consummation at the cross. Without the New Testament, one comes to the end of the Old Testament left hanging in mid-air—what happened to end the story? It's an unfinished book. But when Jesus came, every aspect of the Old Testament suddenly found fulfillment and completion. Now we understand what God was planning during all those centuries.

At the same time, this elaborate typological message validates the entire Bible. How could such a perfectly fitting puzzle have been assembled over the span of two millennia? Jesus' death, with his blood sprinkled before God as the final substitute for all humans, fulfills at one point in time all that the Old Testament had prefigured. This was no coincidence, but the product of direct divine inspiration.

Chapter 11: Implications of the finished work

Since chapter 3 in Hebrews, the argument has been that we should enter God's rest. Remember, God rested from his work because it was finished, not because he was tired. We, too, find rest by entering into the finished work of Jesus.

In Hebrews 7-10, this concept of the finished work of Christ becomes the starting point from which everything else must be measured. As he compares and contrasts Jesus' work with that of Old Testament priests and worshippers, notice how often our author brings up the "once for all" aspect of Jesus' work in the italicized words:

- 7:23-24 Now there have been many of those priests, since death prevented them from continuing in office; but because Jesus lives forever, he has a *permanent* priesthood.

- 7:27 Unlike the other high priests, he does not need to offer sacrifices day after day. He sacrificed for their sins *once for all* when he offered himself.

- 9:12 He entered the Most Holy Place *once for all* by his own blood, having obtained eternal redemption.

- 9:25-26 Nor did he enter heaven to offer himself again and again, the way the high priest enters the Most Holy Place every year with blood that is not his own. Then Christ would have had to suffer many times since the creation of the world. But now he has appeared *once for all* at the end of the ages to do away with sin by the sacrifice of himself.

- 10:10 And by that will, we have been made holy through the sacrifice of the body of Jesus Christ *once for all*.

- 10:12 But when this priest had offered *for all time one sacrifice* for sins, he sat down at the right hand of God.

- 10:14 *By one sacrifice* he has made perfect *forever* those who are being made holy.

You can see from the italicized words how he repeatedly stresses the difference between old covenant sacrifice and the new covenant finished work. These differences point to the urgency of moving on.

Indications of inadequacy

1. Repetition

The first covenant included repetitious ritual, and that in itself was intended to convey a message:

> For the Law, since it has only a shadow of the good things to come and not the very form of things, can never, by the same sacrifices which they offer continually year by year, make perfect those who draw near. Otherwise, would they not have ceased to be offered, because the worshipers, having once been cleansed, would no longer have had consciousness of sins? But in those sacrifices there is a reminder of sins year by year. (Hebrews 10:1-3)

According to this section, God used the repetition to remind people that their problem with sin was not resolved in any final sense; more work was needed. In the meantime, daily and weekly ritual worship reminded the people that the sin problem was hanging over their heads. The result was that each subsequent offering jabbed their consciences with awareness of sin. But with Jesus' single, finished work, things were different:

> How much more will the blood of Christ, who through the eternal Spirit offered Himself without blemish to God, cleanse your conscience from dead works to serve the living God? (9:14)

To have your conscience cleansed means that you live in the confidence that comes from once-for-all forgiveness. The "dead works" here in context mean works intended to relieve one's sense of sinfulness—like the ritual sacrifices the readers were offering.

The NIV and NLT both wrongly take this expression to mean "sinful deeds" or "acts that lead to death." But the author isn't discussing general freedom from sin in this passage. Rather, he is contrasting old covenant works, which are now dead works, with new covenant faith in the finished work of Christ. People who know they are forgiven also realize they don't need to offer any more sacrifice.

Just as these readers were returning to Old Testament ritualism, Christians in the centuries since this book was written have returned to weekly ritual, including offering sacrifice in the mass. Other Christians come to God pleading for forgiveness daily, instead of accepting and believing in Jesus' finished work.

2. Outward sanctuary

As we saw earlier, the tabernacle/temple also conveyed a message of separation, or distance between God and even his own people. While they could approach God carefully, and through a priest, they did not have what our author earlier calls "bold access" (4:16). Thus, in 9:8 the author explains, "The Holy Spirit is signifying this, that the way into the holy place has not yet been disclosed while the outer tabernacle is still standing."

The very fact that people needed a sanctuary implied that they didn't have the kind of union we have with God. In our covenant, our hearts are the sanctuary and true dwelling place of God. Our union with him makes priests, rituals, and outward sanctuaries unnecessary. Christianity is unique in the world because we have no sacred places to revere. In religion, belief in sacred space always accompanies the view that God is dangerous, but also contained to some extent.[29]

Again, Christians from the second century on have tended to return to the idea of outward sanctuary and sacred space. This never should have happened. Just as we saw in Old Testament times, believers are not authorized to decide how they want to approach God. So this reviving of old covenant features like holy places is unauthorized and damaging. When people reintroduce these features, even though somewhat modified, they are doing the same thing the readers of Hebrews were doing.

---

[29] I have discussed the association between sacred space and formalism in general at xenos.org/

Believers from many denominations call their places of meeting "sanctuaries," from a Latin word meaning "holy place." It's common to refer to church buildings as "the house of God"—a term straight out of the Old Testament language of the temple.

People don't realize that regressing to a sanctuary concept is an implicit denial of our intimacy with God. It's not only a doctrinal mistake; it's very misleading to young believers, suggesting what we saw above, that "the way into the holy place has not yet been disclosed."

Single work, eternal effect

Not only was Jesus' work singular and final; the effect of that work on us is singular and final.

> But He, having offered one sacrifice for sins for all time, sat down at the right hand of God.
>
> For by one offering He has perfected for all time those who are sanctified. (Hebrews 10:12, 14)

Both of these statements are important. Verse 12 teaches that Jesus' work was a one-time event with eternal results, but verse 14 teaches us the *effect* of his work on anyone who is "sanctified" (i.e. set apart—the same word from which we get "saint" and a common term for all Christians in the New Testament).[30] Jesus' work "has perfected" all of us permanently and unconditionally. Notice that the verb here is in the perfect tense—a tense meaning already completed action. This perfection is not a possibility for the future, but *an already accomplished fact*.

Many interpreters and church leaders throughout history have shredded the effect of the finished work by suggesting that, while Jesus' work is finished, believers have to access their forgiveness one bit at a time—often with imposing conditions. You might have to go to a priest to confess, be absolved, do penance, and take mass. Or, in other churches, you just might

---

[30] John Wesley misread this verse, thinking that the word "sanctified" referred to Christians who had achieved "entire sanctification" or holiness in their lives. But this passage is not about our behavior, but about our status with God. We are set apart as holy because of our identification with Jesus. This is well-taught in the New Testament. See 2 Cor. 5:21; 1 Cor. 1:8; Phil. 3:9; Rom. 8:1; and closer to our context, the following three verses Heb. 10:15-17.

have to confess your sins to God and ask for forgiveness daily. Either way, this passage and other parallel passages are being ignored, and the believer cannot be confident of where he or she stands with God. Did you forget a sin? What about sins unknown to you? What about the past few hours?

Are you a Christian believer? Then you have already been made perfect. This passage unmistakably teaches that all our sins in the past, present, and future are blotted out at the moment of conversion. You need to believe that in order to have a healthy relationship with God. Believing in total, immediate, and permanent forgiveness is not presumptuous; it's what God wants you to believe. It's the truth. Read verses 15-17 and carefully consider how unqualified and plain the language is.

> And the Holy Spirit also testifies that this is so. For he says, "This is the new covenant I will make with my people on that day, says the Lord: I will put my laws in their hearts, and I will write them on their minds."
>
> Then he says, "I will never again remember their sins and lawless deeds." And when sins have been forgiven, there is no need to offer any more sacrifices. (NLT)

Could any statement be clearer than that?

Chapter 12: Responding to the finished work

Our author has finished his argument. What Jesus did and the Old Testament proof that this was God's plan from the beginning are now clear. But there's more. Now his readers, and we modern readers as well, have to decide to respond in faith.

Whenever God calls on us to do something, we can be sure of three things. First, it's for our own good. He knows what will make us happy and fulfilled. Second, he has already provided a basis for what we are to do. His action precedes ours and makes ours possible. Finally, if we supply the willingness, he will supply the power. All godly actions from us must be empowered by the Holy Spirit.

You can tell our author is referring to God's laying a basis for our action by the 'Therefore... since' language in the following verses:

> Therefore, brethren, since we have confidence to enter the holy place by the blood of Jesus, by a new and living way which He inaugurated for us through the veil, that is, His flesh, and since we have a great priest over the house of God... (Hebrews 10:19-21)

This is nothing but a two-sentence summary of Jesus' finished work as we have seen in the past six chapters of Hebrews.

And then follow five imperatives, or calls for us to take action.

1. Drawing near

> Let us draw near with a sincere heart in full assurance of faith, having our hearts sprinkled clean from an evil conscience and our bodies washed with pure water. (v. 22)

Here is our confidence again—something no Old Testament believer ever would have risked—striding directly through the torn veil into the Holy of

Holies! Our friend, God, is there, eager to welcome us into his embrace. Do you believe that?

Remember, it's not enough just to go into the Holy of Holies. We have to go in *confidently, boldly.* Anything less would be unbelief. Also, the author specifies that we need to draw near with "a sincere heart." That is, we are not to draw near in a formalistic sense, like people do in religion.

Our consciences must be "sprinkled clean," as we saw earlier. Sprinkling is a reference to how the priests would shake drops of blood on the mercy seat. Isaiah predicted of the Messiah that "He will sprinkle many nations" (Isaiah 52:15).

Our consciences won't be clear because we eliminated sin from our lives. Paul explains why we can lose our galling sense of guilt when he says he wants to be found in Christ "not having a righteousness of my own derived from the Law, but that which is through faith in Christ, the righteousness which comes from God on the basis of faith" (Philippians 3:9). When we believe God's new verdict on us—that we are innocent—our guilty consciences can finally be cleansed.

This is why it is so essential that every time we come before God we remember and articulate our position in Jesus. This is "presenting ourselves to God as those alive from the dead" (Romans 6:13).

To have "our bodies washed with pure water" refers to the laver—an oval tub of water in the temple courtyard used by the priests to symbolically wash before approaching God (see Exodus 38:8; 40:30-32). This is another way of saying we are cleansed from sin, reinterpreting Old Testament ritual to fit spiritual experience in Christ.

Jesus has truly prepared the way, but we must rise up and draw near. This drawing near to God will be unclouded by doubt or fear. When we finally and fully believe what Jesus has done, his perfect love will cast out fear (1 John 4:18). Then our hearts can be filled with the love of God in the most direct and intimate fellowship possible.

2. *Holding fast*

Next he calls for loyalty.

> Let us hold fast the confession of our hope without wavering, for He who promised is faithful. (v. 23)

The readers of Hebrews were under persecution (see 10:32-34). It seems like the worst of the persecution was in the past at the time of writing, but more still looms as a possibility. As we suggested earlier, this was probably a key reason the readers were slipping away from faithfulness to the gospel. It was too costly to continue a nonconforming posture with their culture. Another reason was no doubt the same reason people gravitate away from naked grace in many different cultures: the human preference for legalism and self-sufficiency.

We see in this verse God's expectation for them and for us: loyalty to the truth. Any wavering or cowering away from the truth is absolutely unacceptable. We saw that God declared the timid spies and the congregation discussed in chapter 3 to be traitors. When God promises, we are to believe that promise and hold to it with everything we have. Anything else says we don't believe God is faithful. Any such unbelief will be corrosive and ultimately devastating to our relationship with God. Doubting God at one point quickly leads to doubting him at many points.

People under persecution—even when it's no more than being viewed unfavorably—become conscious of their behavior in the presence of their detractors. There is a natural desire to stay under the radar and not attract negative attention. So even in our culture living a life of radical faith and commitment can be an embarrassment to weak Christians. That's when the process of compromise begins.

We see God calling us to hold fast to our hope—a word that refers to future expectation that God will keep his promises. The English word "hope" doesn't convey the clear sense of certainty about the future intended here. This is not hopeful or wishful thinking, but faith directed toward the future with a reliable, promise-keeping God.

This leads to a radical change in values—in our day, probably away from materialistic avarice. In heaven gold is so worthless they use it to pave the streets. Our values cannot remain unchanged when we learn how to hold fast the confession of our anticipation without wavering. Only when we lock our eyes of faith on our future eternal life with God will we have the nerve and desire to give God the loyalty he deserves. Spiritual and even emotional stability come to those who learn to remember daily where we are headed.

3. Focusing on others

The first two imperatives have to do with our relationship with God. Once that relationship is solidly rooted in faith, we become free to turn toward helping others with the spiritual power God bestows. The remaining imperatives are all about how to grow as a community rather than as individuals.

> Let us consider how to stimulate one another to love and good deeds. (v. 24)

This "one-another" passage envisions us getting outside ourselves and taking an interest in the lives of our fellow believers. The one-another language means this is not just for leaders, but for everyone. Consistent with the rest of the New Testament, we are reading that in the body of Christ, our lives are each other's business.

This is completely different than modern western society, where people are expected to "mind their own business" and where privacy has become a fetish. We have to give up the autonomous, individualistic, secret life and give ourselves over to the other people of God to know and be known.

His call is not just to *notice* love and good deeds others do. The point is proactive—I am to spend time thinking about how I can stimulate my friends to excel spiritually. This is the furthest thing from relational passivity. Passive love is selfish love. I wait around hoping someone notices me, and a relationship just happens. If nothing happens I might whine and complain that people aren't loving enough. Passive love: no creativity; no initiative; no thinking through your friends with God; no prayer, or only whining prayer; and no victory.

The imperative word here is not "stimulate," but "consider." The verse is calling on me to spend mental time with God, praying through my friends and considering how I might speak or act in ways that could get them more excited about acting for God. Of course, this implies that I know these people well enough to be in touch with their needs and progress so far. It implies that I have invested in the relationships enough that I enjoy credibility with them. This picture assumes community and discipleship.

People who take this call seriously are on the path to developing personal ministry. And that leads to a new level of joy and fulfillment. Anyone can do it. You don't have to be mature or knowledgeable. You just have to care enough to start building friendships in the body of Christ and then spend time with God, letting him teach you how to become a force for him in your friends' lives.

Ways to stimulate

Think of some of the plans you could lay for talking to people.

- You could notice some area of strength for a friend and suggest he or she try some things to develop that more. Maybe you get him a book on the subject. Or find some good lectures and send her a link.

- Modeling is always a possibility. You could practice behaviors in the presence of others in the hope they will be imitated, and/or share a visionary picture of their possibilities.

- Warning her that a certain sin issue in her life could threaten her progress.

- Go with him to meet his non-Christian friends in the hope of sharing Christ.

- Suggest getting together for a time of reading, sharing, and prayer.

A group where the members are constantly stimulating each other gradually becomes dynamic. It does make a difference. People *feel* connected because they *are* connected. Love comes to love. The true New Testament picture becomes real. But it will never happen if we just sit back and wait. I have to see this as addressed to *me* and take initiative. The details will sort out later, but unless the ship is moving, God won't be able to steer it.

4. Assembling together

Next we read, "Not forsaking our own assembling together, as is the habit of some" (v. 25a). When Christians lose their sense of need for each other, it's always a bad sign. We usually see this loss of normal thirst for fellowship because of apathy, conflict, complacency, worldly time priorities, guilt feelings—in a word, sin.

But there could also be other causes. Some Christians in our world have never experienced real fellowship and don't even know what it is. They may have never been taught that it's biblical and necessary. They may think verses like this one are merely teaching that we should attend a church service. But viewed in its context, this regular "gathering together" is a needed component in the relational framework of the body of Christ.

Every gathering of God's people has the potential to be a major spiritual event, even a life-changing one. That isn't up to a worship band or the preacher. Gatherings of God's people should serve as opportunities to build each other up. Whenever the New Testament gives purpose clauses for why Christians should gather, the reason is to build one another up in the Lord.

Inspiring sermons or performances are fine, but we also need gatherings that are interactive. At smaller, interactive meetings, believers get a chance to use their spiritual gifts. They hang out before and after the meeting so they can reasonably get to know each other and build friendships.

Meetings like these become dynamic when all or most of the believers there come full of the Holy Spirit and watchful for any opportunity to speak or act in a building way. Believers should be praying individually and together before these meetings that they won't go through a whole evening without contributing something elevating.

5. Encouraging

Finally,

> But encouraging one another; and all the more as you see the day drawing near. (v. 25b)

Discouragement is a constant danger for believers struggling through the rigors of spiritual battle, especially when under persecution. One easy way to contribute to other's lives is encouragement. It's free, it's easy, and it often meets some of the most deeply felt needs in others. An encouraging group is a delight to all involved. But effective encouragement is not automatic. Consider some practical points for enhancing your encouragement ministry:

- Encouragement is best with people you know well enough to be aware of their needs, struggles, gifting, progress to date, and meaningful life situations.

- When people live false, double lives before each other, they end up with one's false persona speaking to another's false persona. This cannot result in real encouragement. Read Larry Crabb's excellent book *Encouragement* to learn more about the linkage between authenticity and real encouragement.

- If you know highly encouraging people, watch them when talking to others and imitate.

- Don't flatter. Flattery is complimenting someone unrealistically. Flattery doesn't build people up, and only hurts your credibility. Wait until you can think of something real to encourage.

- Pray about how to frame what you want to say. If you "shoot from the hip" without forethought, it may come out clumsy and vague. This passage calls on us to "consider" before we are in the situation trying to encourage.

- If some tasty scripture fits, that may hold extra weight when encouraging. Reminding people of God's promises is encouraging.

- Mention specifics rather than generalities. Be able to name specific situations or actions that you appreciated or admired.

- Just showing interest in someone's struggles in a particular area can be encouraging. We need to know we are not alone with our struggles and that others care.

- Consider whether to encourage a person privately or in front of others. Sometimes public encouragement is powerful.

- Expressing appreciation for one another is a simple expression of love.

The Big Picture

When we grasp our bold and complete access to the throne of God and draw close to him every day, it frees us from the burden of dead works to enter into valid works: building up the people of God. As we set about the work of developing the community of God's people in an atmosphere of raw grace and regular encouragement, the joy of the Lord is sure to follow.

Chapter 13: The horrific antithesis

After drawing out such an attractive picture of life lived under the complete grace made possible through Jesus' finished work, our author draws a contrasting picture. This picture is neither attractive nor beautiful. It is meant to horrify.

> For if we go on sinning willfully after receiving the knowledge of the truth, there no longer remains a sacrifice for sins, but a terrifying expectation of judgment and "the fury of a fire which will consume the adversaries." Anyone who has set aside the Law of Moses dies without mercy on the testimony of two or three witnesses. How much severer punishment do you think he will deserve who has trampled underfoot the Son of God, and has regarded as unclean the blood of the covenant by which he was sanctified, and has insulted the Spirit of grace? For we know Him who said, "Vengeance is mine, I will repay." And again, "The Lord will judge his people." It is a terrifying thing to fall into the hands of the living God. (Hebrews 10:26-31)

How could he threaten people?

Doesn't it seem strange that after our author spilled so much ink arguing for the safety and security believers in Christ have, he would now introduce one of the most frightening passages in the New Testament?

This passage seethes with menace and threat. Notice the shocking language he chooses: "the fury of a fire which will consume," "terrifying expectation," "dies without mercy," and the final statement, "It is a terrifying thing to fall into the hands of the living God." How is this kind of language to be reconciled with the heavy emphasis on the confidence we are supposed to have with God?

The wrong reading

Many readers take this as the best passage in the New Testament proving that Christians can fall away and lose their salvation if they "go on sinning willfully." Such a view actually leads to the most radical form of falling-away theology—that you could lose your salvation simply by sinning too much. This is way beyond more moderate falling-away theology, where only a deliberate denial of Christ would cause the loss of salvation.

I think the evidence shows that both of these readings are wrong.

First, in sound interpretation we need to follow the thought development in the text, and make sure our interpretation flows right along with that train of thought. The radical falling-away reading fails this test. Instead of flowing with the train of thought development, this reading presents us with a jarring contradiction to what our author has been saying. We suddenly jerk from security to insecurity for no clear reason.

Next, the New Testament teaches that believers are not in danger of losing their salvation, and no book is any stronger on this point than Hebrews.[31] We just studied earlier in this same chapter that Jesus "has perfected *for all time*" those who belong to him (v. 14), and that we should approach God with "the full assurance of faith" (v. 22). Earlier, in chapter 7, we read, "Therefore He is *able also to save forever* those who draw near to God through Him, since He always lives to make intercession for them" (v. 25).

These and other passages in Hebrews rule out the idea that salvation can be lost. At the very least, interpreters who take the view that this passage teaches the possibility of losing one's salvation need to explain how these other passages harmonize with their reading. Merely pitting one passage against another is not valid interpretation. They must show how the passages agree.

---

[31] This is a New Testament teaching not found in the Old Testament. The basis for eternal security is the baptism and sealing of the Holy Spirit. In Jesus' day these ministries still lay in the future (John 7:39). So even during Jesus' life, we cannot assume that believers were safe from losing their salvation.

The real meaning

So what *is* out author saying? The correct reading of this passage shows it is teaching on the psychology of legalism—the mindset that afflicts legalists. It fits perfectly into the argument in Hebrews, standing as a direct antithesis to the security and confidence we have with God.

To understand this reading, consider the following:

- When the author says, "If we go on sinning willfully after receiving the knowledge of the truth" (v. 26) he doesn't mean *any* sin. He means the sin he has been talking about in the context: doubting the finished work of Christ and going back to ritual legalism. This is an important point. This central section of Hebrews isn't about people who cuss too much or get drunk. It's about people turning back to legalism from grace. The first rule of interpretation is context, and the whole book has been arguing against this specific problem.

- Notice the consequence of continuing in sin: not "terrifying judgment" but "a terrifying *expectation of* judgment" (v. 27 emphasis added). He is not arguing that believers are in danger of God's judgment, but that they *think* they are in danger. People under law don't have confidence in where they stand with God. How can they, if their acceptance depends on their performance under law?

- Notice the lurid language our author uses to describe the legalist's state of mind. He fears "the fury of a fire which will consume the adversaries" and other statements we mentioned earlier. They are all deliberately menacing, because his point is that law-living people see God this way. The law is clear: Punishment will be administered for sin. This is the same point John makes when he says, "There is no fear in love; but perfect love casts out fear, because fear involves punishment, and the one who fears is not perfected in love" (1 John 4:18).

- Consider verse 29, where he asks, "How much severer punishment do you think he will deserve who has trampled underfoot the Son of God, and has regarded as unclean the blood of the covenant by which he was sanctified, and has insulted the Spirit of grace?" The extreme language is again evident. The punishment is more severe than death without mercy. He is working his audience into a fit of fear in order to show them where the logic of law leads.[32]

- His main goal comes up in verse 35: "Therefore, do not throw away your confidence, which has a great reward." The danger for this group is not losing their salvation, but losing their confidence before God.

We see a terrible irony with this passage. While the author is trying to warn people away from legalism and the corrosive fear it brings, many readers have turned it into the very thing he is parodying. They think he is actually teaching that Christians are in imminent danger of damnation! Read this way, any Christian could lose his or her salvation accidentally.[33] If you have been under this form of teaching, you should be delighted to learn that this is not the message of the passage.

Grounds for endurance

The author remembers an earlier time when this group was still radical for God:

> But remember the former days, when, after being enlightened, you
> endured a great conflict of sufferings, partly by being made a

---

[32] It is possible to read even this verse as referring to nonbelievers. The "covenant by which he was sanctified" could refer to the fact once people have sat under the preaching of the gospel, they are in a different category from everyone else. This would be the idea of being set apart in a way similar to that in 1 Cor. 7:14, where one's unbelieving wife or husband is "sanctified" (set apart) because they are married to a believer. But he is also clear, "How do you know, O wife, whether you will save your husband?" (v. 16). However, such a reading is unlikely and not necessary in the context of Hebrews.

[33] The radical loss of salvation reading has been adopted by much of the holiness movement (which includes many Wesleyan, Church of Christ, Nazarene, and free-will Baptist or Pentecostal churches, but not all). This is also the view of the Roman Catholic and Eastern Orthodox churches. Based on the number of members in these confessions, this threatening reading, although quite mistaken, is by far the majority reading.

> public spectacle through reproaches and tribulations, and partly by becoming sharers with those who were so treated. For you showed sympathy to the prisoners and accepted joyfully the seizure of your property, knowing that you have for yourselves a better possession and a lasting one. (Hebrews 10:32-34)

You can tell from this passage that the author believes most of his readers are true believers. It's always confusing when people start drifting backward in their Christian walks. The spirituality implied in these verses matches well the early chapters of Acts. Especially impressive is the joy with which they accepted trial and suffering—a sure mark of true faith. But that was before the poisoning turn to legalism put a chill on their zeal for God.

They were under persecution then, and the author of this book may well have been one of the foremost leaders of that attack. Paul admitted that he imprisoned and voted to kill multiple people in Jerusalem. We know he was the primary accuser of Stephen, the first Christian martyr, because people laid their cloaks at his feet as they stoned him to death. He would have also overseen the seizure of their property.

On at least two occasions, Paul led a collection from other groups to help Christians made poor by this attack in Judea. It is not unlikely that this was partly an effort to make right what he had done. From the sound of it, the second collection (discussed in 2 Corinthians 8-9 and the book of Acts) was sizeable.

But the Christians in this group also needed to supply endurance. He goes on to say, "For you have need of endurance, so that when you have done the will of God, you may receive what was promised" (v. 36). Then he goes on to quote Habakkuk 2, which warns against shrinking back, and calls them to "live by faith" (v. 38). The call here is also similar to Jesus' call to the Ephesian church: "Therefore remember from where you have fallen, and repent and do the deeds you did at first" (Revelation 2:5).

The big picture

The message of Hebrews has been consistent throughout. On the one hand is the thesis of all-out grace through Jesus' finished work. On the other hand is the antithesis—the horrifying, soul-chilling return to works. This section teaches mainly on the antithesis, but we can also sense that the author believes his audience are believers and that they are going to listen, as he says in the final verse, "But we are not of those who shrink back to destruction, but of those who have faith to the preserving of the soul" (v. 39).

Chapter 14: Understanding the dynamics of faith

Hebrews 11 is the most complete discussion in the entire Bible on what faith is and how it works. To back up his thesis statement—"Without faith it is impossible to please God" (v. 6)—the author scans over the entire Old Testament!

What is faith?

First come definitions. Hebrews 11:1 is a well known verse: "Now faith is the assurance of things hoped for, the conviction of things not seen."

As we saw earlier, the New Testament word 'hope' refers to our future with God (e.g. Colossians 1:4-5). It does not imply wishful thinking, as our English word hope often does. "I hope it gets warmer soon" doesn't suggest any knowledge that it will get warmer, only that I wish it would. In this sense, hope is a bad translation for this Greek term. It should rather be understood as faith directed to the future—anticipation or expectation. So let's read the first phrase that way: "Now faith is the assurance of things anticipated." The word translated "assurance" here means undergirding or foundation. So faith is the foundation or basis for why we anticipate a future with God.

At point after point in the following analysis of the Old Testament, our author stresses how people of faith don't just live for the present. They live for what they anticipate from God in the future.

Then, too, faith is "the conviction of things not seen." Conviction here means a subjective inner sense that something is true—to be convinced. It can be translated as confidence based on evidence. "Proof" as in the KJV is too strong. Whenever we believe something we can't see, we aren't compelled to believe in some inescapable way. Rather, we choose to believe based on adequate evidence, and then in experiencing God, we add more confidence.

Our author will also contrast the seen and the unseen throughout the chapter. The unseen realm—the realm of God—is just as real as the visible realm of this world. But because it's unseen, only those with faith will live for the unseen over the seen.

Two dimensions

Faith contains both a subjective and an objective dimension.

The objective part is that we believe something that is actually true, even though unseen. This part is essential. Jesus said God seeks those who will worship him in spirit *and in truth*. We are not coming to a God of our own creation, but to the true God as he is.

The subjective part refers to personal trust. With faith, we are believing the truth about God, his word, and his work, but we are also learning to trust him on a personal level—entrusting ourselves to his love and care.

This is what God wants from us. He could have insisted on any number of works—even doing daily push-ups, recitations, or self-punishment. Instead, he wants faith. This is the only thing God can accept from us. If we can only learn to trust him, the rest will come in time. He hasn't called on us to change ourselves. He will bring change in our character when we learn how to trust him.

The author of Hebrews clearly doesn't believe his audience is living in faith. Rather, they are turning to the frequent antithesis to faith—works—and that shift is motivated by unbelief. That's why he feels the need to go in depth about what faith is and always has been throughout salvation history. In this survey of Old Testament history, our author demonstrates what faith is, how it works, and how God responds. Over and over again, we see the heroes of old choosing the unseen over the seen and the future over the present.

Creation

Opening his Bible to page 1, his first observation is:

> By faith we understand that the worlds were prepared by the word
> of God, so that what is seen was not made out of things which are
> visible. (v. 3)

Here is an example of the objective component in faith. How do we know
about creation? We learn that from God's word, which begins with him
speaking the worlds into existence. This creation by command (where God
says, "Let there be light" and there is light) is both unique and amazingly
profound.

Creation myths abound from ancient sources, but none are like the account
in the Bible. Most portray a god going out with ladder, saw, and hammer to
build the world out of already existing matter. Others have mythopoeic
battles between the gods or giant animals, resulting in creation. In Genesis,
the transcendent power in God's word creates something out of nothing.
Only thousands of years later did humans finally confirm that our universe
sprang into existence out of nothing. How could that happen? It did! And
the explanation is the creative power of God's word.

Throughout the Bible, God works though his word. That same word,
whether spoken or written, has power today. But if we want to experience
the full power of the word, we need to believe it.

Abel

From Genesis 1-2, we jump to chapter 4, where we see the first family of
humans and its two sons in action.

> By faith Abel offered to God a better sacrifice than Cain, through
> which he obtained the testimony that he was righteous, God
> testifying about his gifts, and through faith, though he is dead, he
> still speaks. (v. 4)

This verse reveals that the reason God "had regard for" (NASB) or
"accepted" (NLT). God accepted Abel's sacrifice, not because it was a
blood offering (as some teachers have suggested), but because he offered it
in faith. This implies that Cain did not offer his sacrifice in faith. He was
doing something religious for God, but not in faith, and therefore, by
implication, through works.

Cain wasn't trusting and submitting to God from the heart, but deciding on his own what he would do. God knew Cain's bad attitude even though it was invisible to others, but his following actions make his attitude clear. He was angry, jealous, and brooding. God's rejection of works so enraged the religious Cain that he slew his faith-oriented brother.

Hebrews 4:4 has a very cryptic expression in the NASB—that Abel "obtained the testimony that he was righteous" through his offering. NLT says his offering "gave evidence" that he was righteous. NIV says "he was commended." These are all different ways of translating the same word, *martureo* (to give testimony, or to witness), in the passive voice. This much is clear: Abel is not the one witnessing. The passive voice means he is *receiving* the action, not generating it. He is the one being witnessed about, and the one witnessing is God.

Repeatedly in this chapter, this passive use of *martureo* points not to human witnessing, but to God giving testimony in scripture as to what he finds acceptable. The author is proving that coming to God in faith rather than works is nothing new, but has been the message of scripture all along. The summary at the end of the whole list of Old Testament heroes comes in verse 39: "And all these, having gained approval through their faith…." Here again, the term "gained approval" is the same passive use of the word *martureo*.

The author's expression "God testifying about his gifts" means that when Abel offered his sacrifice, God showed (or gave testimony) by accepting it (maybe by burning it, like a later case with Elijah?). This acceptance showed that he was righteous, in the sense that he came to God the right way. Abel's sacrifice was acceptable because he came to God in faith rather than works.

Watch carefully the wording in Genesis 4:4: "The Lord had regard for Abel and for his offering." So it wasn't just the offering that God approved; it was the man. This is how our author knows it was Abel's faith that made his approach to God acceptable.

Enoch

Next comes a man barely mentioned in the Old Testament, but widely admired in Jewish culture because of the pseudepigraphal book of Enoch, which enjoyed a wide reading. Our author doesn't refer to this later book at all. His content all comes from Genesis.

We're now in Genesis 5. The text simply states that "Enoch walked with God" for a long time before he was actually taken by God. This must be what our author is referring to when he says that "he [Enoch] obtained the witness that before his being taken up he was pleasing to God." Here again the scripture "witnessed" (*martureo*) that Enoch was pleasing to God because God took him directly to heaven. That must be the case, because "without faith it is impossible to please Him, for he who comes to God must believe that He is and that He is a rewarder of those who seek Him" (Hebrews 11:6).

Here we have the thesis statement of this chapter. Right at the center of the Hebrews' problem was their failure to realize what God really wants. They thought he wanted more works, more purity, more religion. No. God wants our trust, our faith.

Our author mentions two areas of content to our belief. To believe "that he is" refers to the objective aspect of faith. God's existence and nature are fixed and unchanging and demand belief. Then, to believe "that he is the rewarder of those who seek him" refers to the subjective aspect of faith. If I believe that God is actually happy when I seek him, I am seeing him as good and loving. I'm trusting in him when he promises that he is not annoyed or disappointed when I come to him. It's the same boldness and confidence he's been calling for throughout the book.

Noah

Noah was an incredible example of what radical faith looks like. He must have been a strong believer already in order to stand out against the total corruption that characterized the world at that time. After detailing the universal thirst for evil in the world, Moses says, "Noah found favor in the eyes of the Lord" (Genesis 6:8).

Noah's life took a dramatically different turn when God appeared to warn him of the coming flood and call on him to preserve humanity and animals by building the ark.

The story of Noah is so extreme that even many Christians simply don't believe it is real. If people today have trouble believing in the flood, how much harder would it have been for Noah to believe *before* the flood! Imagine yourself working for a hundred years on an ocean-going barge many miles from the nearest ocean. That truly is "the conviction of things not seen." What a terrible struggle he must have undergone, especially as the years passed and the vision from God moved further and further into the past. But unlike the Hebrew readers, he stayed true to the call and endured, gaining his place in salvation history.

The big picture

In Abel, Enoch, and Noah, we have three primordial men who based their lives on true, heart faith. In each case, the narrative makes clear that God approved of them for that faith and nothing else. Yet, in all likelihood, their neighbors—especially Noah's—probably thought they were crazy.

When Noah constructed the ark, he had no provision for closing the massive three story-tall gang plank/door. Noah had no way to close the door or seal it. Instead, we read the solemn words, "Then the Lord closed the door behind them" (Genesis 7:16). Once that door was closed, it was too late. Unbelief is sealed at some point in time and we no longer have the option of changing our minds. Tragically, while we know our opportunity is limited, we have no way of knowing where that limit is. This underscores the urgency of responding to God in faith "while it is still called 'today.'"

Chapter 15: Abraham

Moving to chapter 12 in Genesis, our writer focuses on Abraham. He is often called the father of faith probably because nearly half the human race look back to him as the origin of their own faith tradition (Christianity, Judaism, and Islam). When Abraham died, the ancient world didn't even notice. But today, he is probably, next to Jesus, the most influential person in human history.

Not knowing

Abraham began his life in Ur but we read, "When he was called, he obeyed by going out to a place which he was to receive for an inheritance; and he went out, not knowing where he was going" (Hebrews 11:8). Here we see a crucial aspect of faith. Abraham took off, not knowing where he was going. Imagine that! You're packing up the family, the livestock, the wagons, and they're asking, "So, where is this place we're going?"

He could only say, "Um... it's that way." He really didn't know.

Most of us resist this. We say we'll follow, but we want to know where God is going to lead us. The issue here is control. When we follow God, not knowing where we're going, that calls for real trust. That requires real faith in the one leading us. But any demand to know where we are going implies distrust. Why do I need to know? What difference would it make if I knew where God was planning to take me? Am I keeping the door open to refuse him at some point? Am I passing judgment on his plans for me? Yes, when we insist on knowing where this is headed, we are not fully trusting.

Action

Abraham didn't merely believe God in his heart. He believe enough to act. No matter what Abraham said or thought to himself, until he put one foot in front of another, faith remained incomplete. The action component of faith—where God always gives us something we can do—completes a spiritual circuit that makes the light come on.

Most of us resist this as well. We want to feel a confident feeling before we actually act. But God works the other way. He knows our faith will never grow if we wait until we feel confident. On the other hand, when we step out on what we know God wants for us, we see him confirm our action and our faith explodes to a new level.

The nomadic lifestyle

We also read, "By faith he lived as an alien in the land of promise, as in a foreign land, dwelling in tents with Isaac and Jacob, fellow heirs of the same promise" (vs. 9-10). In his former life, Abraham was wealthy. This must have been true based on the size of his flocks and having servants later in the story. We also learn through Joshua's prophetic word that Abraham came from an idol-worshipping family:

> Thus says the Lord, the God of Israel, "From ancient times your fathers lived beyond the River, namely, Terah, the father of Abraham and the father of Nahor, and they served other gods. Then I took your father Abraham from beyond the River, and led him through all the land of Canaan." (Joshua 24:2-3)

So the picture here is that Abraham lived in luxury, in the popularity that comes with affluence, and in an environment of false spirituality. These were the "seen" things. The "unseen" things were some land and something about a covenant and a call from a God nobody can see.

Abraham and his family took off. How eerie it must have felt for his family and household. Were they wondering if Abraham had lost his mind? When they finally got to the promised land, nothing changed. He still lived like a nomad, "dwelling in tents, for he was looking for the city which has foundations, whose architect and builder is God (Hebrews 11:10). No brass band greeted Abraham and his household when they got to the promised land. He never lived in a palace, like most great men in history. Instead of his well-appointed house in Ur, he lived for decades in tents, moving from place to place.

He did meet again with God on more than one occasion. The city built by God here refers again to the "unseen." With the eyes of faith, Abraham saw that this would all come out well when God welcomed him into his eternal city. The eyes of faith can see what the carnal eye cannot. Our writer explains:

> All these died in faith, without receiving the promises, but having seen them and having welcomed them from a distance, and having confessed that they were strangers and exiles on the earth. For those who say such things make it clear that they are seeking a country of their own. And indeed if they had been thinking of that country from which they went out, they would have had opportunity to return. But as it is, they desire a better country, that is, a heavenly one. Therefore God is not ashamed to be called their God; for He has prepared a city for them. (vs. 13-16)

Of course they received *some* promises. They had the promised son, Isaac, and the favor and protection of God (cf. Hebrews 6:15). But they never received, for instance, the land they had journeyed so far to live in. Neither Abraham nor his family ever received even an acre of the promised land. When Sarah died, Abraham had to buy a burial plot from an area chieftain.

Neither did they get to see the fulfillment of the Abrahamic covenant. God's word that he would bless all the nations of the world through Abraham wasn't fulfilled for thousands of years. The coming of Jesus, the worldwide spread of the gospel—these would have sounded like pure fiction to this tiny band of wandering nomads. But thank God they believed! God carries forward his work in this world through a string of believing people who all pursue the *unseen* over the *seen*.

Notice, too, that Abraham's faith had to be an ongoing battle, not just one irreversible decision. As the author points out in verse 15, they had the freedom to go back to their homeland at any time. They not only had to go to the promised land, they had to stay there the rest of their days, thus confirming what they believed. This part is particularly applicable to the readers of Hebrews, who were losing heart and giving up their former faith.

Waiting for Isaac

Through most of their story, the greatest faith struggle for Abraham and Sarah was the twenty five year wait for God to keep his promise of a supernatural child.

They wavered at one point, going to a servant girl, Hagar, to fulfill God's will in the energy of the flesh. This was not what God had promised, but instead represented a loss of faith and a consequent felt need to perform works. That's why Paul calls Ishmael (the son Hagar bore) "he who was born according to the flesh" (Galatians 4:29). Sarah's miraculous son, Isaac, meanwhile, was the child of promise—that is, based on faith (Galatians 4:28).

Even though Abraham and Sarah slipped up in this incident, their eventual triumph in trusting God for Isaac is a remarkable story of perseverance in faith. How happy and confirmed they must have felt once their promised son arrived! This is how God grows our faith: He promises, we believe the promise at our current level of faith, he makes us wait, and then answers, resulting in a quantum leap of new faith. The waiting portion is a crucial part of the growth process, and here is where we learn perseverance and endurance.

Paul describes this epic tale of waiting on God this way:

> Without becoming weak in faith he contemplated his own body, now as good as dead since he was about a hundred years old, and the deadness of Sarah's womb; yet, with respect to the promise of God, he did not waver in unbelief but grew strong in faith, giving glory to God, and being fully assured that what God had promised, He was able also to perform. (Romans 4:19-21)

The "seen" in this story was the deadness of Abraham's body and the deadness of Sarah's womb. But Abraham had a promise from God, and he knew God could even raise the dead and that he wouldn't have given the promise if he wasn't willing to use his power to fulfill it.

The ultimate test

But their trials weren't over. In fact, the ultimate test of faith came about 12 years after Isaac's birth. God came to Abraham and said, "Take your son, your only son—yes, Isaac, whom you love so much—and go to the land of Moriah. Go and sacrifice him as a burnt offering on one of the mountains, which I will show you" (Genesis 22:2). How could God ever suggest such a thing? Of course, we now know that God never had any intention of actually letting this happen. Instead, he was planning a remarkable teaching event.

It must have been incredibly clear to Abraham that God's instruction was authentic, otherwise he never would have considered doing it. After all, God himself had promised that this same Isaac was the one through whom he would bless the world. Pondering these two conflicting statements from God, Abraham reached a conclusion that would explain the discrepancy based on raw faith: God must be planning to raise Isaac from the dead after the sacrifice!

> By faith Abraham, when he was tested, offered up Isaac, and he who had received the promises was offering up his only begotten son; it was he to whom it was said, "In Isaac your descendants shall be called." He considered that God is able to raise people even from the dead, from which he also received him back as a type. (Hebrews 11:17-19)

When Abraham took Isaac and parted ways with the other men in the party, he said, "We will return to you" (Genesis 22:5). This is how our author knew that Abraham believed Isaac would raise from the dead. When he took the boy and laid him on the altar, he prepared to strike with a knife. Only then did the angel of the Lord stop him and direct his attention to an animal substitute (Genesis 22:11-14).[34]

I think NASB is correct in translating that Abraham "received him [Isaac] back as a type." NLT and NIV both translate this expression differently (that "as a type" instead means "in a sense"). Thus NLT says "in a sense, Abraham did receive his son back from the dead." But Isaac was a type of Christ in this story, and that makes the most sense.[35] Notice the connections with Jesus' substitution for us:

---

[34] The laws against ever practicing human sacrifice (e.g. Deuteronomy 18:10) came long after this event, so Abraham probably didn't know at this point that God would never allow it. After this event, it was clearer that animal sacrifice stood as a substitute for human sacrifice.

[35] The term is *en parabole*, which usually refers to a symbolic story, like Jesus' parables. The question here is what makes the most sense in the context. "Types" are symbolic events or things that form a predictive picture of God's future actions. The fulfillment event is called the "antitype."

- God stresses, "Take your son, your only son," just like the New Testament stresses that Jesus is God's only begotten son (Genesis 22:2, cf. John 3:16).

- God sends Abraham away from where he was staying to "the land of Moriah" for the enactment of sacrifice (Genesis 22:2). We later learn that this very mountain became the building site for Solomon's temple: "Then Solomon began to build the temple of the Lord in Jerusalem on Mount Moriah, where the Lord had appeared to his father David" (2 Chronicles 3:1). So the very place where the veil was torn in two was also the scene for this symbolic act, carried out a thousand years before the temple existed!

- "Abraham placed the wood for the burnt offering on Isaac's shoulders" (Genesis 22:6), just as Jesus carried the fatal wood for his own crucifixion.

- At the same time, Abraham carried the knife and the fire they would use (Genesis 22:6). So here, just like in the death of Jesus, the father and the son were working together (cf. 2 Corinthians 5:19).

- When Isaac asked where the sacrificial animal was, Abraham answered, "God will provide a lamb, my son" (Genesis 22:8, cf. John 1:29).

So Abraham did receive his son back as a type, or picture, of the son of God who would really, not figuratively, die for human sin.

In this incredible act of faith we see Abraham anticipating that God would come through even if Isaac died. It turned out that wasn't what God had in mind, but he did come through in a different way, so Abraham's faith-anticipation was justified. His fully mature faith resulted in a shockingly accurate prediction of the atoning death of Christ.

The big picture

Abraham's life illustrates every aspect of faith as clearly as any story could. His radical departure from normalcy and worldly security probably looked insane to his neighbors who didn't know God. Cynical observers could easily have concluded that his life was a failure based on materialistic criteria. Still today readers might ask, "Why would I want to live like him?"

A big part of the answer to this question involves something people without God simply can't understand: participation in God's eternal plan. To be used by God as a player in his plan for the rescue of humanity is the most important thing anyone could ever do. Even a million years later, the importance will be undiminished.

God also loved Abraham and took good care of him in this life. Yes, he sacrificed some things, but God also blessed him. At the end of his story we read, "Abraham breathed his last and died in a ripe old age, an old man and satisfied with life; and he was gathered to his people" (Genesis 25:8). How many people could be described that way? God's people know that following him and being loved by him is a blessed life. Any sacrifice he calls on us to make will be far outweighed by his gifts.

Chapter 16: The Patriarchs

In the period after Abraham, the other so-called "patriarchs" continued to live in the promised land, leading a life similar to Abraham's. But we also see a decline in the relative spirituality of each generation until the final one—Joseph—raises the bar back to an amazing height.

Isaac

Isaac isn't discussed much in the text of Genesis. The focus is more on his father, mother, wife and kids. He was a man of faith but doesn't seem to have been a very good leader or teacher.

Jacob, his son, had some very confused views about God and morality. Esau, another son, married Canaanite women and ends up departing the story after selling his birthright. Rebekah, Isaac's wife, is a conniving, lying manipulator who teaches her young son how to cheat and lie. Both Isaac and Rebekah played favorites with their sons. This family was quite dysfunctional, and Isaac has to shoulder much of the blame.

Our author ignores the negatives here and zeroes in on an incident where Isaac demonstrates that he knows God by giving an accurate prophecy of the future. "By faith Isaac blessed Jacob and Esau, even regarding things to come" (v. 20). The "things to come" here refers to his pronouncements that Jacob's descendants would be blessed and Esau's would live in an unfertile land and be subservient to Jacob's offspring (Genesis 27:27-29; 39-40).

These statements were fulfilled when Jacob's descendants became the Jewish people and Esau's became the nation of Edom. Edom wound up inhabiting an area in modern Jordan to the east of the Dead Sea, an area that is arid and very poor for farming. The nation was subjugated by King David and paid Israel tribute money for many years thereafter before they eventually disappeared. Only the Jews still exist today.

Our writer has a simple point here: that Isaac must have been a man of faith, or God wouldn't be channeling prophecies of the future through him.

Jacob

Jacob started out poorly in his biography, but he eventually became a spiritual man. He first appears in the incident where he manipulates his spiritually dense brother into promising him the birthright. We'll discuss that incident in detail later. Next, he deceives his blind father and steals Esau's blessing.

He has to run away to Aram to avoid Esau's vengeance, and there he displays some improving character, but continues in general darkness concerning God. He did poorly as a father, raising a group of thugs that show little regard for God or morality. Jacob's polygamy and favoritism were probably largely to blame for his older ten sons' lack of spirituality, although one son, Joseph, is quite different.

Some of these famous patriarchs lived at a rather low level of spirituality. But it shouldn't surprise us that people in this era were quite ignorant of the nature of God. They had no scripture to turn to, only stories and lessons imparted around campfires or in the home, and any direct revelations God chose to give. It's easy for us to take for granted how fortunate we are to have the full canon of scripture at our fingertips.

Jacob does deserve some credit for raising Joseph as such a spiritual man. Someone must have trained Joseph in faith and the knowledge of God, and it wasn't his mother, who died when he was young.

Our author refers to an incident at the end of Jacob's life where he leaned on his staff and blessed his sons. He does seem dignified in that story, and he, like Isaac, was given several prophetic words from God—including a prediction about Christ.

Joseph

Joseph was man of towering faith, and it is somewhat surprising that he is not given more space here in Hebrews. While most heroes of faith have a dark side as well, that seems to be largely missing with Joseph. His life illustrates all the key dimensions of faith.

Right from the beginning, we can tell God has chosen Joseph for a key role when he gives him accurate, prophetic dreams. Then, when his brothers sold him as a slave, he ended up in Egypt serving a man named Potiphar. Joseph rose to the head of the household through his diligence and the gifting of God. When Potiphar's wife wanted to sleep with him, he could have taken advantage of the situation to rise even higher. Instead, he repeatedly refused, pointing out that it would dishonor God. His refusal to sin landed him in prison.

In prison, he rose to become the caretaker of the other inmates just as he had risen in Potiphar's house. Fifteen years had passed since Joseph's brothers sold him, and there he was still languishing in prison. Later history shows he still faithfully followed God throughout this time. Even though the "seen" was all bad, Joseph was incredibly determined to live for the "unseen."

When two of Pharaoh's key servants landed in prison, Joseph was given divine insight and prophecy. It looked like God might finally be hooking Joseph up with some contacts who could help him, but no. Two whole years pass by with nothing right when he must have felt something was finally happening. Imagine sitting month after month wondering why God wasn't doing anything, wondering where God was, and questioning why your whole life has been a disaster through no fault of your own.

Finally it was time. Pharaoh's butler recommended Joseph as one who could interpret dreams with supernatural insight. Suddenly Joseph was propelled from a dungeon hole to become the second most powerful man on earth! And right from the start, he tells Pharaoh all his insight comes from Yahweh.

Joseph's leadership made Egypt great and later also saved his family, both physically and spiritually. His worthless older brothers were headed down to outright apostasy—falling away from God. The stories in Genesis of their murders, lying, cheating, incest, and intermarriage with Canaanite women are given to show us how poorly things were going spiritually with this family. In all likelihood, the Jewish people would have been assimilated and disappeared within a generation unless something dramatic happened.

Then, because of Joseph, they were able to move to the Nile delta, one of the richest agricultural places in that part of the world. Also, unlike the Canaanites, who were tolerant and very willing to intermarry and assimilate with the Jews, the Egyptians didn't like outsiders, especially herdsmen. The family, which by now included seventy people, was isolated and incubated for over four hundred years in this situation. They came out of Egypt no longer a family, but a nation.

Now we see how misleading the "seen" can be with God factored into the question. This story seems to meander from one disaster to another, but from God's point of view, there was never any doubt about where it was headed. God's unseen plan was unfolding with absolute precision the whole time.

This is an amazing story, but from the faith perspective, the most amazing part is Joseph's faithfulness to God through all those dark years when nothing visible indicated that God was working up to anything. Even *one day* before being summoned to Pharaoh, Joseph had no clue that anything would ever happen beyond those prophetic dreams he had when still a boy. At some point, he put together what God was doing and was able tell his brothers, "As for you, you meant evil against me, but God meant it for good in order to bring about this present result, to preserve many people alive" (Genesis 50:20).

Our writer also points out, "By faith Joseph, when he was dying, made mention of the exodus of the sons of Israel, and gave orders concerning his bones" (v. 22, referring to Genesis 50:24-25). Here at the end of his life, God again gave Joseph the prophetic word, predicting the future exodus.

Joseph also insisted that his body be taken back to the land of Israel. Since he had not lived there long, the only reason for asking to be brought back there would have been loyalty to the covenant. Although the "seen" was Egypt with all her wealth, he was more concerned with the "unseen" Abrahamic covenant.

Chapter 17: Moses

Moses' story begins in the face of harsh persecution, brutality, and mass murder by the most dominant empire on earth at the time. The Pharaoh owned God's people as his slaves. The Jewish people had grown to such great numbers that a new Pharaoh ordered the murder of every newborn male. They seem helpless to escape their ruthless captors.

Birth

That's where our writer begins.

> By faith Moses, when he was born, was hidden for three months by his parents, because they saw he was a beautiful child; and they were not afraid of the king's edict. (v. 23)

Moses' mother hid him as long as possible, but then made the famous basket smeared with pitch. This part of the story is interesting because some portrayals, including what I remember from Sunday school, are wrong.

I always had the impression that they put the baby in the basket and launched it onto the Nile hoping something good would happen. Fortunately, it sailed right to Pharaoh's daughter. So the faith they exercised was a very blind and almost irrational belief that Moses would be saved from this random floating. In fact, what they did was far from that. When she made the basket, Jochebed did not launch it onto the river. "She put the baby in the basket and laid it among the reeds along the bank of the Nile River" (Exodus 2:2). Rather than floating aimlessly, it was lodged in reeds.

Then, they stationed Moses' sister at a distance to watch (v. 3). They knew exactly what would happen next—Pharaoh's daughter came there to bathe. This was no accidental event; they clearly had discovered where she bathed and planted the baby where she would find him. As soon as Pharaoh's daughter found the baby and wanted him, the sister sprang out of hiding and offered to find a wet nurse, his mother. This was all a well set up scheme they had planned out from first to last.

Of course, it was also an answer to prayer beyond anything they could control. They had no way to know how Pharaoh's daughter would respond when she found the baby, so even amidst their planning they faced significant unknowns. But they set up everything so that the only thing missing was God's action.

This is very different from the super-spiritual version of the story where they launch the baby out into the Nile without any plan or preparations, hoping for the best. Instead, this is a good example of the interworking of God's part and man's part in God's service. Faith is not irrational and doesn't prohibit or oppose planning. This example shows that we should plan based on the assumption that God will come through. That way, we are being neither presumptuous nor passive.

At this point in Exodus, God has his man, and he is being raised in the court of Pharaoh himself, benefitting from the best education possible in that day.

Moses' values

At some point, Moses realized who he was and decided to side with the people of God—a decision that would cost him the fortune he could have had as Pharaoh's grandson.

> By faith Moses, when he had grown up, refused to be called the son of Pharaoh's daughter, choosing rather to endure ill-treatment with the people of God than to enjoy the passing pleasures of sin, considering the reproach of Christ greater riches than the treasures of Egypt; for he was looking to the reward. (Hebrews 11:24-26)

Again, we have the "seen" and the "unseen." Moses was "looking to the reward" he knew would come from living for God. What would have happened if he remained a member of Egyptian nobility? Nothing. None of us would have ever heard his name. He would have lived in comfort and died after a pointless life.

Or could Moses have stayed and become a good influence in the Egyptian court? Maybe he could have persuaded them to relax their slavery of the Jews? No. That thought is naive and even foolish. When humans use their ingenuity to figure out how to get God's will done, we are likely to come up with something like: let's win the powerful elite in society, and then they can influence the whole culture for God. Instead, God usually works through the poor and marginal. "Not many noble" was Paul's description of the people of God. Only one being was powerful enough to change Egypt's direction, and he didn't need Egyptian money or influence to get the job done.

Fleshly service

Our author skips over many parts of Moses' story, probably because of space limitations. When we next meet Moses, he is a grown man.

> Many years later, when Moses had grown up, he went out to visit his own people, the Hebrews, and he saw how hard they were forced to work. During his visit, he saw an Egyptian beating one of his fellow Hebrews. After looking in all directions to make sure no one was watching, Moses killed the Egyptian and hid the body in the sand. (Exodus 2:11-12)

This blow Moses struck against the Egyptian empire is frankly pitiful. How is this going to do anyone any good? You can tell it was against his conscience because he looked both ways before killing the man.

This story is a major contrast to the previous one. Here, human agency has run amok. Instead of trusting God, Moses is acting on his own, and the result is miserable. As a result of this action, Moses had to flee Egypt to the land of Midian, where he spent no fewer than forty years pasturing sheep!

Where was God during all these years? Why did he wait so long to appear in the burning bush? The length of time here points to another lesson on faith. God wants to use people to further his cause on earth, but he's willing to take his time. God uses lengthy periods of preparation, and that becomes one of the big trials of faith for many eager servants. It may seem like nothing much is happening. In this story the "seen" is Moses, a man who could have been a wealthy Egyptian noble, walking around in the desert with a small flock of sheep. The "unseen" part is what God is doing in his character. Much needs to be broken and rearranged in all of our lives before we can reach our full potential for God. Many people lose it during this preparation process and turn to other things. Those who endure and wait become God's key players.

Faith and values

What enabled Moses to persevere for so long? We learn that God had revolutionized his values system. He already had chosen "to endure ill-treatment with the people of God rather than to enjoy the passing pleasures of sin" (Hebrews 11:25).

The lifestyle of faith is completely incomprehensible to those in unbelief. What kind of idiot would Moses have to be to pass up one of the greatest careers in the world? And for what? At this time, not even Moses had any idea that he would one day be used to lead the nation to freedom. We search in vain for any external, pragmatic reason behind Moses' action. He abandoned the palace out of faith in some future reward. All the years he persevered with God, he had no idea what the future held for him.

Can you imagine your son or daughter turning down a full scholarship to Harvard in order to serve God in some obscure way? How would you react? Yet even this would pale compared to what Moses did when he turned his back on Pharaoh's palace and wandered off into the desert. As foolish as some might consider that, God always gets the last word.

Moses' victory

In the verses to follow, our author goes on to mention some of the key elements in Moses' triumph over Egypt. Keeping the Passover (v. 28) while God slew the firstborn of Egypt, and crossing the Red Sea (v. 29) while the Egyptians drowned—these were the final acts of God's outward, visible endorsement.

Suddenly Moses' choices didn't look so foolish after all! Now Moses looks very different from the wandering fool in the desert. He is the leader God used to rescue an entire nation; he becomes the instrument of God's revelation of himself to millions through the Pentateuch; he becomes the man who was allowed to stand repeatedly in the very presence of God himself. What was invisible before has now become visible, and anyone with spiritual eyes could now see that Moses was one of the greatest men who ever lived.

Like the other examples in this faith hall of fame, Moses' life illustrates how "that which is highly esteemed among men is detestable in the sight of God" (Luke 16:15). Embarking on a life of honor and glory among fallen humans is incompatible with following God in faith. People who want to follow God must make a conscious choice to turn their backs on the world and all its glories. The path of Jesus included the cross, and if we want to follow him, it will mean the cross for us as well (Luke 14:27).

Here is the mighty power of faith; it sees what others cannot see. Moses' mind was made up once he walked out of the palace and back to the people of God, before he knew that God intended to use him like he did. We have no promise here that such a move on our part will result in our being used like Moses, but we can rest assured that whenever we act in real faith in God, it will result in something awesome.

Chapter 18: Jericho

At this point our author more or less hits the fast forward button on the Old Testament story. But the key themes he goes on to mention are right in line with the picture of faith he has been drawing.

His next example of faith is the fall of Jericho. Here was one of the cities the children of Israel were so worried about when the spies at Kadesh insisted they turn away from the promised land. How is a ragtag band of escaped slaves supposed to overcome a walled city full of trained warriors? Try to build a ramp? Dig a tunnel? Build a battering ram? How about marching around the city six days in a row, and then seven times on the seventh day? While marching, they could periodically blow some trumpets, but nobody was allowed to say anything.

This strategy is beyond absurd. Can you imagine trudging along in the hot sun near the Dead Sea in silence *thirteen times*? Any questions you have about the ultimate purpose of this wild and strange exercise you can keep to yourself, because nobody is allowed to speak a word. We can well imagine the taunts coming down from the wall of the city: "Well come on!! What are you waiting for? Oh, oooh, now they're gonna to blow a trumpet at us!" Your fellow soldiers are glancing at each other, wondering. Just march.

Then comes the seventh day. Jericho would not have been large in area like today's cities. The site today is less than a quarter mile in diameter. But since they had to march outside of arrow range, this march would have been probably a minimum of three miles each time around. Now they're supposed to do that seven times in one day, and then supposedly fight a battle that same day! What kind of preparation is that for a physically demanding fight?

The message of Jericho is crystal clear. God was making double, triple, and quadruple sure these men knew exactly where the victory was coming from. Nobody who experienced this ordeal would ever wonder whether it might have been their own savvy, strategy, and boldness that won the day after all.

As our author argues throughout Hebrews, works and faith are incompatible. God is willing to act, but he insists that we acknowledge it's all of his grace. Any infiltration of works cannot be tolerated, and nothing demonstrates this principle better than Jericho.[36]

And the others, too

Rahab, Gideon, Sampson, and on the list goes. All the way through the Old Testament the principle of faith alone in grace alone prevails. There are no exceptions. Some of the people mentioned lived morally ambiguous lives, but our author's point is that whenever they were used of God, it was because of faith.

In addition to the values theme seen earlier in the chapter, this last section adds the theme of persecution. He mentions mocking, scourgings, chains, imprisonment, people being stoned, sawn in two, tempted, killed with the sword, afflicted, and ill-treated (Hebrews 11:36-37).[37] The faithful life of following God can and does include suffering at the hands of his enemies. The readers of Hebrews had suffered earlier (Hebrews 10:32-34) but have begun to feel like they have had enough. Here our author is using the examples of Old Testament heroes to urge his readers on to perseverance under suffering.

Another dimension of the argument is that such a high price has been paid by those who came before to get to where we are today. Surely we won't refuse to take our turn advancing God's plan for earth, our author urges, even if we, too, have to suffer.

> And all these, having gained approval through their faith, did not receive what was promised, because God had provided something

---

[36] Tragically, and ironically, Joshua's people became self-reliant and complacent immediately afterward during the battle of Ai. They only sent a small force up to fight, they didn't inquire of the Lord about his will, and they were defeated. It also turned out they had a compromiser—Achan—who had stolen booty in Jericho (Joshua 7-8). So in spite of all the measures God took at Jericho to emphasize the need for absolute reliance on him, it didn't work. Because of pride, humans, including followers of God, are always immediately ready to take credit for any victory. Humans prefer works to grace.

[37] "Sawn in two" refers to a pseudepigraphal story about the prophet Isaiah, who they put in a hollow log before sawing the log in half. We are not sure where the story comes from, but it is repeated in the Talmud.

better for us, so that apart from us they would not be made perfect. (Hebrews 11:33-34)

When he says "apart from us they would not be made perfect," he is pointing out that the whole journey of the Old Testament was pointing toward Jesus. He is the culmination and fulfillment of everything the Old Testament believers lived and died for. The expression "made perfect" really means "made complete." We in the body of Christ are here to complete what God is doing on earth—a mission begun in the ancient times, but still incomplete even today.

When he says of the Old Testament saints that they "did not receive what was promised," he doesn't mean they didn't receive *any* of what was promised (see Hebrews 6:15 and 11:33). Rather he means the full promise, the main promise, falls to us.

The big picture

For thousands of years holy men and women have paid the price to advance God's program of rescue on earth. If Jesus had appeared out of nowhere, why would anyone believe in him? It was their expectation of Messiah that made the people open to his coming. The groundwork for Jesus' ministry had been laid.

These heroes of faith lived and triumphed based on key principles that always govern lives of true faith. They lived for the unseen values of God, and they had to forfeit the visible advantages of a life lived for self. It takes courage to go after something none of the unbelieving neighbors or family members see as having any value. People living in faith understand this and boldly volunteer anyway.

The readers of Hebrews were standing on a boundary line, just like we do today. On one side lay faith and the costs that would come with it: community contempt, loss of worldly advantage, and living outside the norms of culture. Of course, they also had God's promise that he would make it all worthwhile, though that promise lay somewhere off in the unseen future. On the other hand, they could turn to present comfort and seeming safety through accommodation with the cultural and religious expectations of their day. They might avoid some suffering that way, even though the spiritual price would be horrific.

Such crossroads decisions separate those who count for God from others who fizzle out pitifully in their Christian lives. Every Christian has multiple opportunities to make these decisions—decisions so important that the alternatives of living for God or settling for compromise dominate the rest of the book of Hebrews.

Chapter 19: The big choice

> Therefore, since we have so great a cloud of witnesses
> surrounding us, let us also lay aside every encumbrance and the
> sin which so easily entangles us, and let us run with endurance the
> race that is set before us. (Hebrews 12:1)

In this famous passage, our author reminds the readers of the "cloud of
witnesses," meaning the heroes of faith he just described in Chapter 11.
This argument would hold so much more force for Jewish readers who grew
up admiring these great figures, but it should hold water for us as well. If
they could live by faith, so can we.

Notice there are two things we need to discard: (1) "every encumbrance"
and (2) "the sin which so easily entangles us."

Encumbrances

These must refer to things that aren't sinful in themselves, because that
would be redundant. If a runner showed up to a race dressed in a heavy
overcoat, jeans, and work boots, his coach would probably protest, "This is
a race, but you're dressed for a day of construction work."

Experience shows that many things could fit into this category. Often,
negative relationships encumber believers. This could have been the case
with the readers of Hebrews. Non-Christian family members can be so
hostile to your spiritual growth that you reach a point where you have to
make a decision. When Jesus said, "Unless you hate father and mother...
[you] cannot be my disciple," he didn't mean people should hate their
parents. It's an idiom meaning to love them less than they loved God. He
was speaking in a day and a culture where parents might very well disown a
child who followed Jesus. The same may have been true with the readers'
friendships or community ties that would suffer if the readers got serious
about their faith.

Today, relationships still often effectively block growth. That girlfriend or
boyfriend, certain family members, or longtime friends may act like a ball

and chain in your life. Just as Abraham had to go out from his people, we might have to make a similar decision.

Today in the West, our encumbrance might be something as trivial as a hobby or sport. Americans spend copious time and money on obsessive pursuit of excellence in their workout regimes, video games, fashion, beauty, or knowledge of every sports statistic. Such extreme expenditures of time and mental effort are encumbrances that make real progress in spiritual growth or ministry virtually impossible.

Sin

Some people think that Christians under grace won't have sufficient motivation to escape from sin habits. Not true. Believers living under grace are far more likely to gain freedom from sin than are legalists.

People under grace know that sin poses a mortal threat to their spiritual growth, their ability to lead successful lives, and their ability to carry out the mission God has given them. Instead of being afraid of what God will do to them if they sin, grace-based believers avoid sin because it is so incongruent with the relationships they are developing with God and others. Instead of worrying about others' judgment, grace-oriented believers don't want to squander their lives on sin and miss being a part of advancing God's plan on earth.[38]

The race

Paul talks about running a race as a metaphor referring to one's ministry. That's probably how our author is using it here as well. New Testament writers never view the Christian life as an end in itself. God rescued us so we can pour our lives out for others.

Clearly, the race is long distance. God can't use sprint runners. Very little that we seek to develop in ministry is quick. Building healthy local bodies

---

[38] It's interesting to see here the language about "laying aside" (*apotithimi*) sin, so typical of Paul's thinking (c.f. Colossians 3:8; Ephesians 4:25). In Paul's theology of spiritual growth, we lay aside the old nature with its evil practices like we would lay aside a dirty old coat. Such things simply don't fit with our new identity in Christ. Also reminiscent of Paul is the following statement about running a race with endurance (c.f. 1 Corinthians 9:24-27; 2 Timothy 4:7). Paul is alone among New Testament authors in using this imagery.

of Christians is long-term work. Discipleship is long-term work. Even seeing our own character change is a long-term project (as we saw earlier with Moses, Joseph, and the others).

The readers of Hebrews lacked endurance. They had started so well, but by now it was evident with them, as with so many others, that a great beginning doesn't necessarily mean a good finish. In the author's view their running is woefully inadequate. Real progress in the Christian life and in ministry are only available to those who go all-out for God. Offering God the leftovers is an insult, and God won't honor it. God is God, and he expects to be treated as God, not as an afterthought or a compartment in our lives.

Set before them

Our author's language here implies that God has set out a specific plan for people's lives. Like a cross-country course, the runner has to stay on the path if he wants to win.

We know Paul viewed his own and others' lives this way. He says, "I have competed well; I have finished the race; I have kept the faith!" (2 Timothy 4:7 NET).[39] Finishing the race here implies that Paul believed God had a specific plan for his ministry. He also tells Timothy to "fulfill your ministry" (2 Timothy 4:5), an expression that implies the same thing for Timothy. In Ephesians 2:10 he taught that we are all "His workmanship, created in Christ Jesus for good works, which God prepared beforehand so that we would walk in them." Whether or not Paul wrote the book of Hebrews, it's clear that our author holds the same view.

Notice, the fact that God has a plan for our lives and service doesn't mean we are in any way fated to carry that plan out. To the contrary, these statements clearly imply that it's all too possible to miss the opportunity to complete our course. Otherwise there would be no reason to write the passages.

---

[39] I agree with the NET Bible here that the first phrase should not be translated, "I have fought the good fight," but rather that "I have competed well." This is the literal meaning—to strive or to compete, not necessarily to fight.

God offers you the amazing opportunity to live your life as he planned it. That plan is perfect for you—taking into account exactly who you are and how you are wired. But if we choose the tragic path of preferring our own plan to his, we will suffer the fate we choose.

People worry about accidentally missing God's plan for their lives, but this isn't a real danger. If we are willing, God will make sure we learn his will in time to act on it. If we are confused on some parts, we will at least know other parts that provide a forward path within our ability, and that in turn will lead to our discovering the rest of what he wants us to know.

God promises, "I will instruct you and teach you in the way which you should go; I will counsel you with My eye upon you" (Psalm 32:8). The idea that someone could be doing his best to discover and follow God's will and accidently miss it reflects a mistaken view of God's character. He is neither weak nor unloving in a way that would make such a mishap possible.

Eyes forward

> …fixing our eyes on Jesus, the author and perfecter of faith, who for the joy set before Him endured the cross, despising the shame, and has sat down at the right hand of the throne of God. For consider Him who has endured such hostility by sinners against Himself, so that you will not grow weary and lose heart. (Hebrews 12:2-3)

I never ran many long races, because I was a cigarette smoker from the age of 11. But I could make it 100 yards down the track. You quickly learn that you can't look around to see how everyone else is doing. Your only chance is to rivet your eyes on that finish line and bear down. And if you're like me, you're going to find out soon enough how others are doing when they pass you by.

Fixing our eyes on Jesus is a theme found in all New Testament books. Paul, Peter, and John are strong on it. Having a Christ-centered mindset is powerful and life changing. To be Christ-focused, we have to look away from our performance, from the law, from the past, from our failures, from our circumstances, and from the world. Here is one of the great struggles in the Christian life. Read Romans 8:5-6 and count how many times Paul uses the terms "mind set on the spirit" or "mind set on the flesh." According to Paul, the mind is the true battlefield in spiritual growth.

From verse 2 we learn that Jesus is the author of faith. That's true for four reasons.

(1) Nobody would ever believe in Jesus unless God drew him (John 6:44, 65). Because our fallen natures are depraved, we are simply unable to respond to God apart from a supernatural intervention by the Holy Spirit.

(2) Jesus is the initiator "in that while we were yet sinners, Christ died for us" (Romans 5:8). Humanity never called out to God suggesting he send the Son as an atoning sacrifice. No such thought ever entered any of our heads. God has always been the initiator. He still is.

(3) The Lord bestows faith on his followers. According to Paul, "God has allotted to each a measure of faith" (Romans 12:3). That doesn't mean some get faith and others don't. The language here is clear that "each" means each and every person receives faith. When you think about it, everyone, even non-Christians, have faith. They just aren't placing their faith in God. Neither is the amount of faith we have static. Faith can grow (1 Peter 1:7), and we can pray for more faith (Mark 9:24). In this sense, Jesus is also the perfecter of our faith, whether through trials or through directly bestowing additional faith.

(4) Jesus is the author of faith because he supplied the supreme example of what it means to deny self, ignore his fears and agony, and still go forward to the cross. With Jesus' sacrifice we see the same elements of faith we saw in Chapter 11. Here the "seen" was his agony, shame, and the hatred of his enemies. The "unseen" was "the joy set before him." Jesus' joy came in part from his love for the millions he would save through the cross; also that he would soon "sit down at the right hand of the throne of God."

No wonder our author urges his readers to "consider Him who has endured such hostility by sinners against Himself, so that you will not grow weary and lose heart" (Hebrews 12:3).

The big picture

It's doubtful that most Christians view their lives as a race. For too many, their Christian lives are a source of comfort and blessing, but nothing as intense as a race. Adopting the race perspective would lead to a radically different picture of Christian living. Racing is rigorous, intense, even exhausting. Runners are completely absorbed by their races.

Entangled and encumbered believers, on the other hand, soon decide that the idea of a race is way over the top. It's just too extreme. A little jogging might be alright, but this idea of stripping down to shorts and track shoes for an all-out race, ignoring or discarding so many of the cool things in life, is simply too much to ask or expect.

Of course, these same encumbered believers have lost effectiveness in their ministries if they ever even tried to build one. They are not experiencing the joy of the Lord that comes to fully committed followers, and in their hearts they know they are rationalizing a half-hearted walk with God.

We should note that it's the author of Hebrews—a real champion of grace—who thinks long-distance racing is a good picture of the Christian life. Grace doesn't lead to the kind of passivity in view here. Grace is exciting, energizing, and motivating. Giving your all to your race is not legalism, as some suppose. On the contrary, it's the only reasonable response for one who really knows God (Romans 12:1-2).

Chapter 20: A father's discipline

Woven throughout the text of Hebrews is the background of persecution. Although we can't tell how severe the persecution was at present, it was definitely severe earlier (Hebrews 10:32-34). And, we've seen hints that avoiding persecution was one of the key motives for accommodating the gospel to ritual Judaism.

So, it's not surprising to see the author turn to a discussion of suffering. The desire to avoid suffering is natural, but also overlooks crucial biblical teaching—namely that suffering is one of God's key means of growth. The readers' misinterpretation of suffering is a major contributing factor to their spiritual defeat, as the author points out.

> You have not yet resisted to the point of shedding blood in your striving against sin; and you have forgotten the exhortation which is addressed to you as sons, "My son, do not regard lightly the discipline of the Lord, Nor faint when you are reproved by Him; For those whom the Lord loves He disciplines, And He scourges every son whom He receives." It is for discipline that you endure; God deals with you as with sons; for what son is there whom his father does not discipline? But if you are without discipline, of which all have become partakers, then you are illegitimate children and not sons. Furthermore, we had earthly fathers to discipline us, and we respected them; shall we not much rather be subject to the Father of spirits, and live? For they disciplined us for a short time as seemed best to them, but He disciplines us for our good, so that we may share His holiness. All discipline for the moment seems not to be joyful, but sorrowful; yet to those who have been trained by it, afterwards it yields the peaceful fruit of righteousness. (Hebrews 12:4-11)

Suffering and spirituality

Most Christians have heard teachings on how suffering is good for spiritual growth. But the evidence often demonstrates that we either don't believe the teaching, or that we place little value on growing spiritually.

Notice several points in the passage above.

First, he points out that their suffering has not yet reached a point where their blood is being shed. Although believers had been killed earlier in the Jerusalem group (including recently their leader, James the Just, in 62 A.D.), the readers were not among those who had shed blood (and if Paul is the author, he may not have known about James' death). That's probably true for most of us as well. How many of us have shed a single drop of blood from persecution? For most of us, disapproving glances or, at the worst, harsh language are about all we've had to endure. A few Christians in the West lose jobs, or even have their family disown them because of their faith, but that's still relatively uncommon.

Not so in much of the rest of the world. According to the 2015 Open Doors World Watch List, "The year 2014 will go down in history for having the highest level of global persecution of Christians in the modern era."[40] Death, imprisonment, beatings, and other horrors await Christians in many parts of the world today. One Christian in China was recently quoted as saying that they pray persecution won't end in China, because then they would lose their zeal and become like the church in America.[41]

Our author is suggesting that his readers are soft. Unlike the Old Testament believers who suffered in the most horrendous ways, the readers of Hebrews, and most of us today, are radically underestimating what suffering for our faith entails. I know of times when I've complained bitterly for nothing more than a dreary feeling or lack of excitement. Compare that with the hair-raising list of torments at the end of Hebrews 11.

---

[40] J.C. Derrick, "Open Doors: Worst persecution yet to come," *World Magazine*, Jan. 7, 2015. Africa is rapidly rising in the ranks of persecution, but the Middle East is still the worst.

[41] Paul Hattaway, http://www.historymakers.info/sermons/paul-hattaway-interview.html

Secondly, he warns against "regarding lightly" (v. 5) the discipline of God. To regard lightly probably means indifference, or a failure to see the spiritual import beneath suffering. People regard God's discipline lightly when they attribute their suffering to circumstances or other people, and completely fail to see what God is doing. For many, the question never comes up. Fleshly minded believers have only the predictable responses to suffering—how to get out of it, and bitterness at the apparent causes.

A third possibility is that people "lose heart" (v. 5) when being corrected by God. Here is the enemy's charge: God has forsaken you; he's given up on you. Fatalism and hopelessness are like poison to real faith, and that's why our enemy is constantly pressing such conclusions on us. Yielding to this thinking for a single minute could be spiritually fatal. His lies never come alone. As soon as you believe one, he will have a follow up suggestion that fits perfectly with what you just believed, and another after that. The place to stop this sequence is at the beginning!

The fourth response is the right one: realize that "the Lord disciplines those he loves" (v. 6). People who trust God actually give thanks during trials. Here is the great divide between belief and unbelief. Deep knowledge of God comes to those who grow for years in his grace. With every passing year we should be gaining deeper insight into his loving work in shaping our character.

When we choose not to give thanks in suffering, it triggers a sequence of cynicism. Our eyes become blinded to the hand of God and we become obsessed with how to avoid further suffering. The pain of suffering is actually magnified to the unbelieving mind. The pointlessness and randomness of suffering under the unbelieving mentality make it almost unbearable.

By contrast, suffering in faith becomes surprisingly easy. We come to have Paul's perspective—that his sufferings were "momentary light affliction" (2 Corinthians 4:18). It's not only that we realize our trials will change our lives for the better. It's also that our knowledge of God's goodness refutes the sense of meaninglessness people get when suffering in unbelief.

God's will and suffering

Particularly with persecution, it would be wrong to think God necessarily causes the suffering, even though he takes credit for it (as in this passage). God's "permissive will" means that he has the ability to stop all suffering, and yet he doesn't. Therefore, in a sense, "those whom the Lord loves He disciplines." The immediate cause could be the reality of living in a fallen world—Christians get sick and die just like other people. Or, in the case of persecution, the hatred of those persecuting, and Satan's agitation may be the immediate causes.

But for us, all sufferings can be blessings from God, badly needed to keep us from the consequences of a non-suffering life. Imagine what we would be like if we never suffered: spoiled, selfish, self-reliant, and proud. Suffering is not optional in the Christian life. Our fleshly nature and habituation are too strong to yield to anything less than significant suffering.

God offers the antithesis to unbelief: "All discipline for the moment seems not to be joyful, but sorrowful; yet to those who have been trained by it, afterwards it yields the peaceful fruit of righteousness" (Hebrews 12:11). Notice that the kind of righteousness God imparts isn't the self-righteousness that just creates anxiety and comparison with others. It's the peaceful fruit of true humility which loses self in the love of Jesus.

Resisting trials

Resisting or resenting suffering is really a form of revolt against God, although those rebelling seldom see it that way. The ungrateful sufferer is really saying that God's promise to conform us to Jesus' image through suffering is a lie. Lack of thankfulness plainly says God doesn't have our best interests at heart and has abandoned us.

These little battles over willingness to suffer in faith can be more important than you realize, and can change your life permanently. Our author warns of this in verses 12 and 13:

> Therefore, strengthen the hands that are weak and the knees that
> are feeble, and make straight paths for your feet, so that the limb
> which is lame may not be put out of joint, but rather be healed.

Imagine breaking your leg in the ancient world. Not good! They knew how
to set simple fractures, and they knew how to use splints, which would be
similar to our casts, though far less effective. But healing a fracture was
always dangerous. If a "doctor" came in to set your fracture, he would give
no local anesthetic as we know it. You might get a good slurp of wine and a
leather strap to bite down on. The key was to hold still and let the doctor
work.

It would hurt like nothing you ever experienced. But if you thrashed around,
the "limb which is lame" might be "put out of joint." In other words, you
could end up with a compound fracture beyond their ability to fix. Many
people in the ancient world hobbled about on crutches for no other reason
than they could not hold still and let the doctor work.

The spiritual analogy is clear. When God brings or allows suffering to come
into your life, it's because your limb is lame. It needs repair, and that's
going to hurt. But remember, things could get worse! Running or otherwise
avoiding suffering can easily turn a problem that God could have repaired
into one that could ruin your life, and even the lives of others.

This last possibility comes up in verse 15:

> See to it that no one comes short of the grace of God; that no root
> of bitterness springing up causes trouble, and by it many be
> defiled.

In the context, the bitterness here probably refers to the readers becoming
bitter about their own suffering—including bitterness at their persecuting
neighbors and bitterness against God himself. This is probably the best way
to understand verse 14, " Pursue peace with all men, and the sanctification
without which no one will see the Lord."

He's not threatening them with damnation if their lives aren't holy enough
(a legalistic reading embraced by a surprising number of commentators).
What would such a threat have to do with seeking peace with all men?

Rather, he has in view the conflict and persecution lying behind this whole passage. By pursuing peace even with their persecutors, they will demonstrate the "sanctification" in their lives (i.e. lives that are changed and different than others). When they demonstrate the reality of Jesus through peacemaking, others outside the group will see the Lord through them (see the *very* similar argument from Paul in Romans 12:18-21).

A case in point

To remind his readers how bad things can get, our author refers to the story of Esau:

> Make sure that no one is immoral or godless like Esau, who traded his birthright as the firstborn son for a single meal. You know that afterward, when he wanted his father's blessing, he was rejected. It was too late for repentance, even though he begged with bitter tears. (Hebrews 12:16-17)

At first glance, this recounting makes it sound like the readers might end up like Esau: a man who went too far. Any chance he had for repentance passed by, resulting in doom. That would be a virulent threat indeed! In fact, it is a virulent warning, for them and for us, but not that bad.

Esau was Jacob's older brother—by only a few minutes, but that mattered. Because he was technically the older brother, he had the so-called "birthright." In this case, the birthright was not only the right to inherit the larger part of the family livestock and wealth. It also included the right to inherit the special covenant between Isaac and God—a unique place in the plan of God.

To some people, having a place in God's plan of rescue for the world wouldn't mean much, maybe nothing at all. But to people who know God, nothing in this world matters more than what God is doing.

One day Esau came home hungry from a failed hunt. There, he saw his brother Jacob cooking some stew. He pleaded for some, but Jacob wouldn't give any up unless Esau agreed to sell his birthright in exchange. Esau reasoned, "Behold, I am about to die; so of what use then is the birthright to me?" (Genesis 25:32). His proposition wasn't very plausible. He didn't seem like a man about to die, but maybe in his mind that was believable. In any case, he made the deal, and the solemn word of commentary comes from scripture, "Thus Esau despised his birthright" (Genesis 25:34).

This last statement leaves no doubt about how God viewed Esau's action. Yes, he might have been hungry, in pain, uncomfortable, but none of these justified what he did. Later evidence shows he never intended to keep the deal anyway. But God was listening! When Esau acted, God saw something dark in his heart. Esau's immediate comfort and avoidance of suffering meant more to him than the priceless birthright of Abraham's covenant with God. Notice some key points in this story:

- The soup was immediate. Any value having to do with this covenant thing was way in the future. Or, we could say, the soup was the "seen" while the covenant was the "unseen."

- The soup probably tasted good, especially to a hungry man like Esau. His immediate hunger was satisfied.

- He made the decision under duress. If he hadn't been so hungry, he probably wouldn't have made the same decision.

- Nobody but Jacob was watching, so he could always deny it later (or so he thought).

- There was bread, too! Esau would probably want this point included on the list.

- Esau's brother was unloving, selfish, manipulative, and dishonest (as becomes clear later in the story), so he was guilty too.

- Esau made his choice freely. Nobody forced this decision from him.

- The satisfaction from the soup was only temporary. Esau would have to eat again, while the covenant with God was eternal.

Notice carefully the results of his decision:

- He ate the soup and bread and was satisfied

- He did *not* lose the family property and wealth. This part probably should have happened, but it never did.

- The spiritual part of Esau's decision turned out to be *permanently binding*! This was true even though later history shows he didn't realize it was binding at the time.

This last point is deeply troubling to people who care about God. Running away from a trial might not have as much impact as this one did for Esau, but you never know. When Esau realized his decision had been frozen in time, resulting in his father refusing to give him the family blessing, he wept uncontrollably. We read that "he cried out with an exceedingly great and bitter cry" (Genesis 37:34), but nothing could change the past. Esau's loss was permanent; the Jews would descend from Jacob.

As far as we can tell, Esau went on to live a normal life from the viewpoint of the world. He must have been prosperous and influential in order to later come riding out to Jacob at the head of 400 men (Genesis 33:1). Esau's problem wasn't physical or material. It was spiritual. He forfeited his role in God's plan.

The readers of Hebrews were in danger of suffering the same fate. Avoiding suffering wouldn't cost them their salvation, but it could permanently reduce the role they could have played in the drama of God's redemptive plan for humanity. To people who understand what God's plan is, that would be a tragedy.

We, too, will have plenty of opportunities to opt for a bowl of soup in place of being used by God. Not all of our decisions to avoid suffering will have the kind of impact Esau's did. But it's always dangerous to presume on the grace of God.

Avoiding suffering by compromising our faith is not something you just do once. It's habit forming, blinding, and compounding. If avoiding suffering worked one time, why wouldn't it work another? And in cases where we can't see any immediate consequences, it's even more dangerous. Remember, Esau had no idea that his agreement to buy soup that day would have the impact it did. Imagine how he feels about that decision today!

Chapter 21: Sinai or Zion?

> For you have not come to a mountain that can be touched and to a
> blazing fire, and to darkness and gloom and whirlwind, and to the
> blast of a trumpet and the sound of words which sound was such
> that those who heard begged that no further word be spoken to
> them. (Hebrews 12:18-19)

Every feature of this mountain is frightening. Blazing fire, blasting trumpets
so loud the people at Sinai begged for it to stop. Our author goes on:

> They could not bear what was commanded: "If even an animal
> touches the mountain, it must be stoned to death." (v. 20)

This is holiness—the untouchability of God. God stands in such
transcendent awesomeness that neither people nor even beasts can approach
him without death. Sinai is the place where God gave the law. Fire, dark
clouds, a roaring voice; these were so scary that we read, "The sight was so
terrifying that Moses said, 'I am trembling with fear'" (v. 21). Moses was
close to God if anyone was, but even he trembled at this picture.

This is what the readers of Hebrews needed to see. God is not the
diminished being of the Pharisees' creation. Even touching God's mountain
meant immediate death. God is so righteous and powerful that even Moses
himself, a true holy man, was deeply shaken by the idea of approaching him
in his own works. What chance do we have?

Nothing is scarier than coming before God in ourselves, and this whole
picture of Mount Sinai is intended to stress that point. That's why the most
important words in this paragraph are, "You have not come to [such a]
mountain!" (v. 18). By going back under law, the readers were choosing a
road leading only to fear and alienation. Who can be close to God under
these conditions?

The good news follows:

> But you have come to Mount Zion, to the city of the living God,
> the heavenly Jerusalem. You have come to thousands upon

> thousands of angels in joyful assembly, to the church of the
> firstborn, whose names are written in heaven. You have come to
> God, the Judge of all, to the spirits of the righteous made perfect,
> to Jesus the mediator of a new covenant, and to the sprinkled
> blood that speaks a better word than the blood of Abel. (Hebrews
> 12:22-24)

The contrast couldn't be more extreme. Mount Zion, where Jerusalem was
built, was the scene of God's answer to his own justice: the death of Jesus.
Joyful angels and people who have attained the status of being "the
firstborn" are an inviting picture. God is still the judge, but there's no
problem, because who is he judging? The "spirits of the righteous made
perfect"! And, of course, we are coming to Jesus, the mediator of a better
covenant.[42] Just as Abel's blood cried out from the ground for God to judge
Cain's murder, Jesus' blood cries out forgiveness—"a better word" indeed.

What a spectacular contrast, and how perfectly it exemplifies the whole
point of this book! God gave us law to show us our problem. He never gave
it as the way to relate to him. For that, only grace will do. Law leads to
distance from God as well as dishonesty, demoralization, and apostasy.
Grace leads to love and intimacy with God.

The final warning

For the last summary in Hebrews 12 we turn to the much more readable
New Living Translation:

> Be careful that you do not refuse to listen to the One who is
> speaking. For if the people of Israel did not escape when they
> refused to listen to Moses, the earthly messenger, we will certainly
> not escape if we reject the One who speaks to us from heaven!
> When God spoke from Mount Sinai his voice shook the earth, but
> now he makes another promise: "Once again I will shake not only

---

[42] This contrast between Jerusalem (or Zion) and Horeb (or Sinai) is remarkably similar to that used by Paul in
Galatians 4:21-31, where Horeb stands for the law and Zion for grace. He also refers to "the Jerusalem above"
(Gal. 4:26). This again suggests Paul's influence over the book of Hebrews. The early church also saw the New
Jerusalem descending from heaven to earth in Revelation 20, probably because of the millennial passages in the
Old Testament (in my view, exemplifying those promises, not replacing them). So Paul was not the only one who
used this simile, but this passage in Hebrews is extremely similar to Paul's use.

the earth but the heavens also." This means that all of creation will be shaken and removed, so that only unshakable things will remain. Since we are receiving a Kingdom that is unshakable, let us be thankful and please God by worshiping him with holy fear and awe. For our God is a devouring fire. (Hebrews 12:25-19)

The basic point here is that just because God has fully revealed his grace in Jesus, it would be a huge mistake to think that makes him soft. God is just as much the judge of the universe as he ever was. If anything, the clarity of his offer of grace makes people more accountable than ever, just as remembering his judgment makes grace more highly valued. Jesus is coming back, riding at the head of the heavenly hosts to claim what is his.

People who view God's grace as a turn to weakness and universalistic acceptance of anything couldn't be more mistaken. Grace cost Jesus his blood in withstanding the judgment of God. Thousands paid with their lives, often in gruesome suffering, to complete this marvelous plan of rescue. The explosion that was grace literally rocked the heavens and the earth—and it's not over! The Old and New Testaments alike insist the day is coming when "every knee shall bow and every tongue confess that Jesus is Lord, to the glory of the Father" (Philippians 2:10-11; Isaiah 43:23; Psalms 86:9).

We can only appreciate the value of grace when we consider the horrific price God had to pay for it. We will never fully understand what God did for us at the cross. And that sacrificial love makes turning away from pure grace the most despicable insult we could ever hurl at God! Our author could hardly use stronger language here in warning that forsaking grace is no small matter.

Chapter 22: Living out grace

Some legalistic thinkers fear grace because they think people under radical grace will go crazy with sin. Without the fear of punishment, what is to keep people from indulging every urge of the flesh? This fear is mistaken.

Instead of a careless shrug of moral indifference, our champion of grace ends his book with a string of powerful reminders that a true understanding of grace makes believers *more* eager to follow God's pathway of love. Imperative after imperative follows, all perfectly in harmony with grace. That's because grace gives us the freedom to admit our failures as well as the power to succeed. In new covenant logic, I follow God's will not in order to be accepted, but because I already am accepted.

Love of the brethren

Hebrews 13:1 says, "Let love of the brethren continue." Here is the familiar term *philadelphia*—brotherly love. The first fruit of grace is the ability to take one's eyes off of self and one's performance before God and others, as God's love breaks into the heart with incredible force. As John frankly puts it, "We love because he first loved us" (1 John 4:19).

The result is a spiritually-inspired ability to love at a level never known before. Christians living under grace have the opportunity to experience true body life. The shared mystical union with Jesus leads to a new way of thinking, unencumbered with judgmental compulsions that inevitably result from performance orientation. Love replaces competition.

Some Christians wonder why they haven't experienced this kind of love, and the most common answer is that they aren't living under grace. Legalism is a love killer of the first order. Other things can also kill real love—like versions of love that are soft, unwilling to discipline each other for their own good, or more focused on feeling loved than on giving love. But the premier slayer of true love in Christ's body is legalism, so the follow-up verse makes clear sense.

Love of the others

> Do not neglect to show hospitality to strangers, for by this some
> have entertained angels without knowing it. (Hebrews 13:2)

In English it's hard to see how this verse follows from the previous one, but
not in Greek. Love of the brethren is *philadelpha*. Verse 2 is *philaxenia*.
The word *xenoi* means "strangers." So the author is saying, "Keep loving
believers and also those outside the body of Christ."

Viewed this way, the usual English translation "hospitality" is weak, in my
opinion. This verse isn't just suggesting that we entertain people; it's calling
for a much higher concept—that we love those who aren't part of the "holy
huddle" of believers.

Today, hospitality may mean nothing more than having the neighbors over
for a cookout, even though you might hold some of them in contempt. The
concept of loving the outsiders is much more rigorous and sacrificial.
Loving those who share our worldview and values is so much easier than
loving the raunchy "sinners" around us. But grace calls us to love those who
don't know Jesus. Those who have received God's grace cannot help but
long for others to experience that grace as well.

When the author says, "for by this some have entertained angels without
knowing it," he is probably referring to Bible stories like that in Genesis 18,
where Abraham shared dinner with two angels and Jesus himself! That
happened again with the men on the road to Emmaus (Luke 24:13-35).
Orthodox Jews still leave an empty chair and the door ajar on Passover, in
case Elijah shows up. Tradition teaches that he will come on Passover, and
dine with a righteous Jewish family.

Remember the prisoners

> Remember the prisoners, as though in prison with them, and those
> who are ill-treated, since you yourselves also are in the body.
> (Hebrews 13:3)

This verse has spawned many prison ministries, and that's a good thing,
even though it's not what he's talking about. This community was under
persecution, and that often involved imprisonment. Notice the last phrase

"since you yourselves are also in the body." These were Christians imprisoned for their faith.

Visiting a Christian prisoner was dangerous. If the pattern in this day was anything like that in Acts 8, the authorities were actively searching for Christians to persecute. Visiting a known Christian in prison could easily throw suspicion on you. Yet, unless free people came and supplemented the miserable food portions of bread and water in ancient prisons, the prisoners could waste away.

The same applied to those being ill-treated. These might have been believers who lost their jobs or were more or less excluded from the larger community because everyone knew they were Christians. To associate with them—to go to their house or have them to your house—showed everyone that you were probably a practicing Christian also.

So this verse is really calling for solidarity under persecution. Love in the body of Christ has to be willing to risk persecution.

Marriage held in honor

> Marriage is to be held in honor among all, and the marriage bed is to be undefiled; for fornicators and adulterers God will judge. (Hebrews 13:4)

Marriage is the acid test of love. A relationship this intimate cuts through any effort to hide the truth about ourselves. Every immaturity, every jealousy, every act of selfishness, and every loss of temper rocks our marriages. Especially in the modern world, marriage is up against imposing barriers never known in the ancient world. Youth workers today are aware that the majority of high school boys and a growing number of girls are completely addicted to pornography. Sending one another pictures of their genitals is considered normal.[43] And often these activities are going on right

---

[43] Experts say the average age of first exposure to pornography is continuing to fall and is currently around 11 or 12 years old. http://national.deseretnews.com/article/802/-Adolescent-addiction-When-pornography-strikes-early.html#5khsomICOFkJE5Iq.99 The *New York Times* reports, "For teenagers, who have ready access to technology and are growing up in a culture that celebrates body flaunting, sexting is laughably easy, unremarkable and even compelling." http://www.nytimes.com/2011/03/27/us/27sexting.html.

under the un-seeing eyes of mom and dad. How successful do we think porno addicts are going to be in marriage?

The church must truly hold marriage in honor today if we are avoid the outright failure in marriage going on all around us. Couples will need help before marriage and afterward. Although sometimes exaggerated, the divorce rate is climbing steadily among Bible-believing Christians. The church today (including the one I'm in) is not successfully resisting the cultural norms that work against good marriage.

Notice that fornication is just as much a part of this picture as adultery. The author here insists that sex be reserved for marriage. Even modern Christians agree adultery is a serious betrayal, but too often, modern churches look the other way when it comes to fornication before marriage. In one large church after another, couples are fornicating and the church adopts a "don't ask, don't tell" policy.

American Christian parents continue to urge their marriageable children to wait until they are out of school and financially established to get married. With the average age at time of marriage now hovering around twenty-eight years old, young people are being asked to go through the most robust, sexually-charged decade of their lives as singles. The result is predictable: fornication. And nobody seems to care. Sociologist Mark Regnerus shows that the marriage age among Christians is almost the same as non-Christians, and that their rates of fornication are almost the same as well.[44]

The Christian church today is in a spiritual battle for the integrity and durability of marriage. When our author says God will judge fornicators and adulterers, he is probably referring in most cases to passive judgment. In passive judgment, God simply refuses to protect us from the negative consequences of our sin. In the case of sexual sin, the consequences are likely to be severe. Losing your family will be the biggest horror of your life if it happens. To evade that fate, it's well worth any effort to avoid marriage killers involving sexual sin.

---

[44] "Over 90 percent of American adults experience sexual intercourse before marrying... The percentage of evangelicals who do so is not much lower... just under 80 percent." The same with marriage age. Mark Regnerus, "The Case for Early Marriage," *Christianity Today*, Aug. 2009.

Free from the love of money

> Keep your lives free from the love of money and be content with
> what you have, because God has said, "Never will I leave you;
> never will I forsake you." So we say with confidence, "The Lord is
> my helper; I will not be afraid. What can man do to me?"
> (Hebrews 13:5-6 NIV, quoting Deuteronomy 31:6 and Psalm
> 118:6-7)

Each of the previous imperatives relates to practicing sacrificial love toward
fellow believers, toward outsiders, toward the prisoners, and toward
spouses. Why suddenly bring up the love of money?

One reason is the corrosive effect money love has on real love. With
materialistic avarice, we begin looking to things instead of relationships for
fulfillment and happiness. This fundamentally wrong-headed turn is much
more dangerous than most people realize.

Lust for money—and the toys, treasures, and honor that come with it—is a
bottomless hole. Like all addictive things, money lust delivers stimulation,
but never satisfaction. What seemed to be exciting at one point quickly
loses its thrill, leaving gnawing hunger in its place. Pursuit of more money
usually comes at the direct expense of our relational lives with God and
others. These are the dynamics of addiction.

But lust for pleasure and admiration aren't the only reasons people turn to
money. Notice how our author rebuts the love of money by quoting God
saying, "Never will I leave you; never will I forsake you," as well as
another passage from Psalms about God being our helper so we won't be
afraid. By answering money lust with these passages our author points the
finger on another big reason people turn to money: security and safety.

Our culture (just like theirs) lingers long and hard on the idea of "financial
security." Wealth management companies continually imply that you must
be crazy if you don't have a million or more laid up for your luxurious
future. They constantly remind us of all the things that could go wrong and
insist that having more money and diversified investments is the answer.

Christians who fall for these arguments are distrusting God. They are
looking to the "seen" instead of the "unseen." That's how dullness of

hearing and hardening of the heart begin. We may whisper that we trust
God, but our actions shout unbelief. All our priorities shift once any love of
money slips in. So insidious is the entrance of this sin—and so numerous
are the specious arguments to cloak the love of money in respectability and
even virtue—that we must view it as extraordinarily dangerous.

Remember what our author gives as the antidote: Jesus' assurance: "Never
will I leave you; never will I forsake you." Yes, the one thing that can
deliver us from the love of money is the assurance of his closeness and
eternal acceptance. To have God himself near us, loving us, that is true
security money can never deliver.

Contentment

Paul calls contentment "the secret" that brings happiness into all of life
(Philippians 4:12). Contentment is nothing less than faith. When we really
trust God, we realized that no matter what circumstance comes, God must
think it's OK. Therefore, if I know God, I think it's okay, too.

Contentment is a thankful refusal to rebel against the life God has given. In
place of anxiety and lust for what we don't have come joy and gratitude for
what we do have. We begin to develop something extolled throughout
scripture: true appreciation for the awesome gifts of God. So many of our
emotional problems can be healed through deep appreciation of God that
it's almost impossible to exaggerate its importance. If you're struggling
with the love of money (or its sister, anxiety), pray from your heart that God
will teach you this precious virtue.

Chapter 23: Living out grace in the church

Along with the New Testament version of salvation and spiritual growth comes the New Testament picture of the people of God as a community. Just as the old covenant has been utterly superseded on spiritual growth, it has also been superseded in understanding of community through the body of Christ.

The church in the New Testament (i.e. after Pentecost) is very different from God's people in the Old Testament. With the coming of the Holy Spirit, who unites us with Jesus and carries out his new ministries, a whole new understanding became necessary. No longer are the people of God trying to organize a theocratic government and state. No longer do they fight wars with their neighbors. No longer do they punish wrongdoers with death or slavery. No longer are they under orders to stay away from their neighbors or to kill them (Deuteronomy 7:2-5). Some might think this list too obvious to mention, but in fact, Christians have mistakenly attempted every item on this list throughout the history of the church. Trying to bring in Old Testament law to direct the operation of the church would be just as big a mistake as bringing in law for the doctrines of salvation.

Instead of pursuing these misguided ends, new covenant people are sent out into the world to associate with sinners, love them, and win them to faith. Unlike ancient Israel, entry into the people of God comes exclusively through conversion, never through birth (John 1:13). Believers' time together no longer involves going to holy places, but rather building each other up and using their spiritual gifts—a teaching not found in the Old Testament.

Imitate

> Remember your leaders who taught you the word of God. Think of
> all the good that has come from their lives, and follow the example
> of their faith. (Hebrews 13:7)

By the time Hebrews was written in the 60s A.D., many of the original
leaders in this church were probably dead. As those who followed God to
the end, the believers now realize how wise their leaders' direction was as
those leaders revel in the presence of God.

The heroic champions in the New Testament become our pattern to copy as
well. The standard for spirituality is noticeably higher in the New
Testament than in the Old, which makes sense because we have the
universal indwelling of the Holy Spirit and ready access into the Holy of
Holies itself. In a healthy church today, our leaders should be the kind of
people we can point to with confidence and suggest that people study their
way of life and imitate their faith.

Avoid the esoteric

> Jesus Christ is the same yesterday, today, and forever. So do not
> be attracted by strange, new ideas. Your strength comes from
> God's grace, not from rules about food, which don't help those
> who follow them. (Hebrews 13:8-9 NLT)

The NLT correctly shows the connection between verses 8 and 9. Since
Jesus hasn't changed at all, and never will, our teaching shouldn't be
changing either. Esoteric teaching is when leaders claim to have some
special insight that nobody else has. The church has been plagued
throughout its history by people offering such teachings. Joseph Smith and
Mormonism would be an extreme example, but many other examples
haven't broken away from mainstream churches—they just corrupt those
churches from within.

People can undermine Jesus' teaching in more than one way. Some do so by
simply denying what he says. Others add to his teaching by bringing forth
additional sources of authority. This latter has an insidious undermining

effect just as bad as outright denial, as the second authority set up next to scripture always becomes the true authority in the end.

One alien authority church leaders frequently roll out is the Old Testament, improperly applied. The old pattern of worship and the clergy/laity distinction, altars, robes, priests, holy days, and sanctuaries have all reappeared in the church, taking it far away from the picture we have in the book of Acts and the epistles.

And don't miss which direction the negative, false, and strange teaching takes—*always away from grace*. Our author clearly suggests this by the alternative he gives: "It is good for the heart to be strengthened by grace" (v. 9). Instead of being strengthened by grace, the readers were apparently still fussing with dietary laws. These were not only completely pointless, but also showed a fundamental confusion about where they are in God's plan (Mark 7:19). As we have seen throughout, this group was stuck in the old covenant.

In Christian history this tendency has been very predominant, even in completely Gentile groups. Already in 95 A.D. Clement of Rome, writing our first extra-biblical Christian source, makes most of his points on leadership from Old Testament teaching on priests. Then throughout the second century, we see a growing Old Testament mindset in the writings of the early fathers. Priesthood was reintroduced, and the New Testament teaching on every member ministry disappeared. Ritual grew extravagantly in prominence. Within another century, altars, incense, priestly robes (like the Old Testament ephod), and scores of other formalistic features took over people's thinking and practice in the church.

But far worse than any of these was the loss of grace teaching. Christians were taught to seek forgiveness week by week through cleansing rituals and penance. By this time, they were just as far out as the readers of Hebrews. To be praying to Mary and saints; to believe in purgatory; and to urge "almsgiving, indulgences, and works of penance undertaken on behalf of the dead"[45] surely would fit the description of being "carried away by varied

---

[45] *Catechism of the Catholic Church*, Second Edition III, 1032.

and strange teachings." The finished work of Christ was trampled horribly when the church departed from radical grace.

Once they abandoned the authority of the New Testament in favor of the Old, how surprised can we be that they ended up torturing and burning people at the stake? Fighting religious wars fit with the Old Testament, and they justified it using obsolete Old Testament passages. At a time when European peasants were constantly on the verge of starvation, the church could think of nothing better to do with its fabulous wealth than build immense cathedrals (consciously based on the Old Testament temple) that sometimes took over a hundred years to build using thousands of workers every year. What is wrong with this picture? It's a classic case of human preference for strange and varied teachings instead of having their hearts strengthened by grace.

Chapter 24: Going outside the camp

We have noted several times that the readers of Hebrews were under persecution and rejection from their own society. Their culture was highly religious which is often the worst kind of society when it comes to persecution.

In our culture, rejection, criticism, and scoffing also hurt. But one danger appears in softer rejecting cultures like ours: Believers might conclude that we are close enough to cultural acceptance to make full acceptance a plausible goal. Those in countries where persecution is harsh, like India or China, know there will be no acceptance from majority culture, and they don't waste time trying to gain it.

What are Jesus' followers to do according to the book of Hebrews? The answer is very uncompromising: We must forget about being accepted and determine to deliberately bear our culture's reproach.

As an illustration, the author again brings forward the Day of Atonement prescribed in Leviticus 16. In our passage, he calls attention to how the carcasses of sacrificial animals were taken outside the camp and burned (Leviticus 16:27). He sees that as symbolic of how Jesus was driven outside the city for his crucifixion. And at a deeper level, this lonely rejection from the city becomes a picture of our own need to forsake any thought of being accepted by the world system.

Jesus' view was no different:

> If the world hates you, keep in mind that it hated me first. If you belonged to the world, it would love you as its own. As it is, you do not belong to the world, but I have chosen you out of the world. That is why the world hates you. (John 15:18-19 NIV)

Any time the world doesn't hate us, it's probably because we have accommodated so completely that they no longer see any point in worrying about us. That's exactly how they treated the false prophets, according to Jesus (Luke 6:26). We must be willing to "go out to Jesus, outside the camp, and bear the disgrace he bore" (v. 13). In the readers' case this meant no longer accommodating to Old Testament ritualism and legalism. That is often the case with us as well. To go outside the gate will often mean leaving our legalistic religious tradition in favor of a more radical following of Jesus.

When our author points out, "We have an altar from which the priests in the Tabernacle have no right to eat" (v. 10), he is pointing to the utter incompatibility between our covenant and the old covenant. Our altar is so far superior to what they had that it's unthinkable that we would ever go back. The old priesthood has no part in the sacrifice of the cross, the new worship should have no part in the old sacrifices.

Our version

Anyone engaged in evangelism today is familiar with people thinking, "I get this feeling Jesus is real, but if I accept him, I'll be rejected by my family." We see this sentiment (not always stated so directly) whenever Muslims, Jews, Hindus, or even people from some "Christian" denominations consider giving their lives to Christ. This was certainly the case in Jesus' day. Families might actually never again talk to a member if he or she followed Jesus. This culture was not tolerant in any sense.

In our secular world today, the goal of gaining the world's acceptance is equally incompatible with following Jesus. Often parents and others have no problem with your announcement that you believe in Jesus. It's not until the things of God become a priority, even interfering with all-out pursuit of career and money, that the sparks begin to fly. Our modern world will harshly persecute those who put God ahead of worldly goals.

Scripture explains the concept of forsaking the world's approval in different ways, but all of them are very strong. In Romans 12:2 Paul says, "Do not be conformed to this world, but be transformed by the renewing of your mind." This is a conscious either/or decision that every believer has to make and reaffirm—conformity to the world, or transformation from the Lord. Which will it be?

James is even stronger: "You adulteresses, do you not know that friendship with the world is hostility toward God? Therefore whoever wishes to be a friend of the world makes himself an enemy of God" (James 4:4). He calls them adulteresses because they are betraying their betrothal to Jesus in favor of a world system deliberately set up by Satan to lead people away from God. Through James God insists that no compromise on this issue is possible. Following Jesus won't lead to approval from the world. It will lead us outside the city gates.

When living under rejection and persecution, we have to remind ourselves constantly that we will share Jesus' glory in heaven, but we will share his rejection until then. This is why our author says, "For this world is not our permanent home; we are looking forward to a home yet to come" (Hebrews 13:14).

Chapter 25: Updated sacrifices

We have seen that for Christians, offering any kind of atoning sacrifice to God is an insult to Jesus' finished work. But what about the other sacrifices in Old Testament worship?

Thank offerings

Many offerings at the tabernacle were not for sin; they were 'thank offerings' or 'peace offerings.' These were simply a way to say "thank you" to God. Old Testament believers saw these sacrifices as ways to worship God. Most words translated "worship" mean to serve, but several key words almost always mean doing the temple or tabernacle service.

It turns out we can still offer thank offerings under the new covenant, but our thanksgiving sacrifices have changed:

> Through Him then, let us continually offer up a sacrifice of praise to God, that is, the fruit of lips that give thanks to His name. And do not neglect doing good and sharing, for with such sacrifices God is pleased. (Hebrews 13:15-16)

The word for sacrifice here is the same one used throughout the Bible (including the Greek version of the Old Testament) referring to ritual sacrifice. But we don't offer animal or grain sacrifices anymore. Instead, he has reinterpreted Old Testament worship into new covenant forms, giving us three "sacrifices" we can offer God.

Appreciation

The first offering he mentions is praising God. When we praise God, we are merely acknowledging the truth. (The phrase "give thanks to his name" should read "confess [*homologeo*] his name.") When we face the facts about what Jesus did for us, the normal response is praise. We don't need an animal; we just lift up our hearts to God in wonder and thanksgiving.

Amazingly, we read that "God is pleased" when we do this. It's not that God needs people to praise him so he can feel good about himself. Rather, it makes him happy to see that our attitudes are turning away from the selfishness and rebellion that lead to ingratitude.

Ungrateful Christians are one of the most puzzling pictures we could ever contemplate. Ungrateful Christians are being so narcissistic that *even the cross isn't good enough!* Even undeserved eternal salvation isn't a good enough gift to make us thankful. How shocking our fallen natures can be!

Creatures this blind, this darkened, and this selfish seem like they would be beyond the pale of those God can love—but we're not. Instead, God urges us to open our eyes, to admit (confess) or acknowledge who he is and what he has done, and then let fly our praise and thanksgiving. "With such sacrifices God is pleased," because we are turning away from the ugly narcissism of all-out selfishness to the truth—and that is going to be very good for us. Instead of destroying ourselves with a grotesque fixation on what we don't have, we will be uplifted and become happy by facing and acknowledging what we do have. This is true worship of God.

We could offer our thanksgiving and praise through song or prayer, but we can also do so in other ways.

Doing good

Next comes the simple idea of doing good. It's not complicated because the concept is so broad. It simply means that when we acknowledge God's grace and we want to show him our thankfulness, we should do something good with the mindset, "God, I'm doing this for you." This is called serving (or worshipping) the Lord.

In many cases, doing good involves serving others—that is what we call ministry. Paul considered his ministry to be like an Old Testament thank offering:

> The grace that was given me from God, to be a minister of Christ Jesus to the Gentiles, ministering as a priest the gospel of God, so that my offering [sacrifice] of the Gentiles may become acceptable, sanctified by the Holy Spirit. (Romans 15:15-16)

When Paul calls himself "a minister of Christ," he doesn't use the usual word for minister. Instead he calls himself a "liturgist"—a worship leader. This is New Testament worship: loving others sacrificially, including sharing the gospel with them, and serving them in the name of Jesus.

Koinonia

The final mode our author suggests for worshipping God is translated here "sharing." That is a possible translation for the Greek word *koinonia*, but the majority New Testament translation for this word is "fellowship."

If the author means sharing here, then he is probably referring to financial giving to the poor and to the work of God as a form of worship. Financial giving is a thank offering to God, and well-pleasing to him. This would accord with other passages teaching that new covenant worship often takes the form of financial giving. Notice how Paul refers to a financial gift from Philippi as "a fragrant aroma, an acceptable sacrifice, well-pleasing to God" (Philippians 4:18). Here again, giving has replaced Old Testament ritual offerings.

If, on the other hand, *koinonia* here means fellowship, the sense is broadened to include more acts of sharing and ministry that should be a part of fellowship. Fellowship in the New Testament involves the gathering of God's people to build up one another. The New Testament epistles contain over fifty "one another" passages detailing how Christians can build each other up.[46] Most of these passages are simply detailing the central imperative from Jesus that we love one another.

What is love in the New Testament context? Certainly it is not mere sentimentality, let alone the eroticism, usually ruling in our culture. The New Testament brings a special take on what real love is. We don't have space to go into detail on this, but to summarize, under Jesus' new commandment—that we love one another as he loved us (John 15:12)— believers take it upon themselves to make each other's growth and progress their business. Unlike modern culture, where individualism and privacy

---

[46] For a detailed explanation of the one-another passages, see Gary DeLashmutt, *Loving God's Way: A fresh look at the one-another passages*. (Columbus OH: New Paradigm Publishing, 2015).

reign, the body of Christ is a community in which our lives are each other's business and in which we commit ourselves to give sacrificially to build each other up. Every act, every word intended toward that end is an act of worship, according to this passage.

So our author brings forward three distinct ways to worship God (praise, ministry, and fellowship, or giving) but none of them involve a worship service. That's because the worship service concept is an Old Testament idea, never taught in the New Testament.[47]

A false dichotomy

You might have heard or read teachers making a dichotomy, or contrast, between worshipping the Lord and doing ministry or outward deeds of service. The argument runs that too many Christians are focused on things like ministry and serving, or on other believers. Instead, they should be going inward to seek out deep "worship" experiences.

Here, in Hebrews 13, you see how wrong such divisions are. Inner experiences of the joy of the Lord are good, and we saw that praising God was one important channel for worship. But outward giving in sacrificial love is just as important, and takes nothing away from other ways to worship the Lord. In fact, unbalanced worship that only focuses on one's self and God quickly becomes individualistic and really selfish. In time it implodes, as spiritual unhealthiness results in spiritual eroticism—the vain search for ever more stimulating experiences with God.

Healthy worship involves both a vertical and a horizontal dimension that enhance and fortify each other. Any failure to develop both dimensions in your own life and the life of the church will lead to spiritual stalemate.

Follow your leaders

> Obey your leaders and submit to them, for they keep watch over
> your souls as those who will give an account. Let them do this

---

[47] Engaging with God; Worship by the book

> with joy and not with grief, for this would be unprofitable for you.
> (Hebrews 13:17)

Throughout the history of God's dealings with humans, he has worked through human leaders, including in the New Testament church. Human leadership doesn't contradict the Lord leading the church; it should facilitate his leadership.

One pattern of leadership changes significantly from the Old Testament to the New: In the New Testament local church we see plurality of leadership. This was virtually unknown in the Old Testament, where leaders were nearly always singular men or women (like Deborah) called by God to their roles as king, charismatic leader (Moses, the judges), high priest, or prophet.

Israel did have elders in towns and villages in Old Testament times, mainly for deciding legal cases. Later, after the exile, they often gave elders a role in their synagogues, and New Testament eldership may be loosely based on that.

The twelve apostles served as elders in Jerusalem (notice how Peter calls himself an elder 1 Peter 5:1). Although Peter, and later Jesus' brother, James, served as apparent senior leaders, they consistently worked with a group of leaders. When Luke refers to leadership decisions, he portrays them as corporate decisions made by the apostles or elders thinking together (e.g. Acts 6:2; 15:22).

Later, wherever church planters chose elders, they always appointed plural elders in each church—even when the groups were new and small (Acts 14:23; Titus 1:5). Peter says the elders (plural) should shepherd the flock (singular) of God among them (1 Peter 5:1-2). Apostles, on the other hand, continued the Old Testament pattern of singular charismatic leadership although even they tended to work together in apostolic bands, like we see with Paul in Acts.

The New Testament also teaches that leaders are accountable not only to co-leaders, but also to their members' clear reading of scripture. When Jesus warns his future followers to "Beware of the false prophets, who come to you in sheep's clothing, but inwardly are ravenous wolves"

(Matthew 7:15), he puts the burden of discernment on each and every one of us. We cannot trust any elite caste of theologians to assess the validity of church teaching.

Later, Paul echoes this when he says the church should "let two or three prophets speak, and let the others pass judgment" (1 Corinthians 14:29). In the Spirit-empowered new covenant church, common members are fully capable of using scripture and good discernment to judge false teaching when they hear it.

So the obedience to leaders here is never un-contingent or unconditional. We should only follow leaders to the extent they follow Christ (1 Corinthians 11:1).

Chapter 26: Closing words

We have reached the end of the letter. In the closing verses, notice a few more interesting points.

> Pray for us, for we are sure that we have a good conscience, desiring to conduct ourselves honorably in all things. (Hebrews 13:18)

This reference to the author's confidence in his "good conscience" reminds us of the apostle Paul, who stands alone in making similar statements in the New Testament (Acts 23:1; 24:15; Romans 9:1; 2 Corinthians 1:12; 1 Timothy 1:4; 1:19; 2 Timothy 1:3). The verse also raises the likelihood that the author is working with someone else. The "we" here points to a possible co-author, which might again help to explain the difference in style between Hebrews and other books by Paul.

Goodbye

> Now the God of peace, who brought up from the dead the great Shepherd of the sheep through the blood of the eternal covenant, even Jesus our Lord, equip you in every good thing to do His will, working in us that which is pleasing in His sight, through Jesus Christ, to whom be the glory forever and ever. Amen. (Hebrews 13:20-21)

This sign-off (theologians like to call it a benediction, but it's really just a prayer of blessing) is very similar to others by the apostle Paul (e.g. Romans 16:25-27; Ephesians 6:23-24; 2 Thessalonians 3:16-18). He prays for their equipping for ministry and stresses that God will work in us what he wants to see. Just as this whole book has stressed the absolute need to depend on God's grace alone, here at the end we see that there is never a thought about equipping or enabling oneself. We must see that all our ability comes from God, and that's the only way all glory can be his.

The notice about Timothy is significant. "Take notice that our brother Timothy has been released, with whom, if he comes soon, I will see you"

(v. 23). This not only shows that the author is in Paul's immediate circle; it also shows that this book must have been written after the end of the book of Acts. Acts never mentions Timothy being imprisoned, or him and Paul planning a trip like this when he gets out. This scenario simply doesn't fit into the story in Acts. Therefore, Hebrews must have been written between the end of Acts, (at least 62 A.D.) and the Jewish revolt against Rome (66 A.D.). If the author of this book was Paul, he was near the end of his life, although he had no way to know that. He was captured in the persecution Nero launched against Christians in Rome around 65 A.D.

We already saw that the author's greeting to their leaders along with "those in Italy" who are with the author, suggests the author is in Italy, and argues *against* the idea that he's writing *to* Italy as many commentators argue.

Finally, the expression, "Grace be with you" fits Paul's practice perfectly. (e.g. Romans 16:23; 1 Corinthians 16:10-20; 23; 2 Corinthians 13:13-14; Philippians 4:21-23; 2 Timothy 4:19-20; Philemon 23-24).

Aftermath

The Jerusalem church wasn't to last long either. When the Jews in Palestine rose in revolt against Rome in 66 A.D., many Christians remembered Jesus' warning to flee if they saw Jerusalem surrounded (Luke 21:20-22). Eusebius says their flight and refusal to fight further embittered the Jews.[48] But for the Christians, it mean life. Many fled to the east and formed Jewish Christian communities in a number of cities in what is modern day Jordan and Syria.

So, sadly, we don't know exactly what effect the book of Hebrews had on the group. But the fact that it was respected enough to be considered scripture suggests strongly that the author got through to a significant number in the group. More important is that the book has ministered to millions in the centuries since, leaving us in no doubt about where we stand in relation to the old covenant.

---

[48] Eusebius, *History of Christianity*, III:5. Other early historians mention it as well, but might get their information from Eusebius.

In retrospect, only a situation like that which existed during these few years between the book of Acts and Paul's death would have elicited a book like Hebrews. Now it seems clear that God used this small historical window to settle once and for all how to understand the relationship between old and new covenants, and indeed how to understand our relationship with God.

The ultimate recipients of this letter were not the Jerusalem church, but ourselves. With Hebrews in our canon, all the books in the Bible cohere in a way they never would have without it. No longer should there be any confusion about how extreme God's grace is, or how boldly we may come to him.

Also by Dennis McCallum:

Have you ever wished you had a short simple book you could hand to a non-Christian friend who is willing to explore the claims of Christ? *Discovering God* is the book. In easy to read prose, McCallum lays out the case for Jesus' and the Bible's authenticity.

McCallum's most popular book was co-authored with his daughter, Jessica Lowery. In *Organic Discipleship* the authors expound their combined 60 years experience in fostering a disciple making church.

Walking in Victory is a study on spiritual growth as taught in Romans 5 through 8. This passage is easily the Apostle Paul's most complete discussion on the subject. Easy to read and highly practical, this title breathes God's grace.

What should a real Christian community look like? What should its ethos be, and how in particular should it function? How does one discern God's vision for such a body of believers? If you are interested in these kind of questions, then Dennis McCallum's *Members of One Another* is the book for you! Dr. Ben Witherington

Balanced, non-sensationalized study of Satan, his character, and his kingdom—the world-system. Learn it all from Genesis to Revelation.